ENDORSEMENTS

In a day and age plagued by medicated phobias, natural calamities, economic collapses and unprecedented diseases, *Bulletproof* sets the stage for a people to become unbreakable in the face of intimidating evil. In this powerful and long-overdue book, Jeff Rostocil shares insights for victorious living and maps out blueprints for living fearlessly. As the three Hebrew boys were able to withstand the fiery furnace and come out unscathed, the revelation of Psalm 91 unlocked in this book will become a shield for believers to withstand the fiery furnaces of their day. It is one thing to have a revelation but quite another to become the revelation, and Jeff embodies Psalm 91. His experience has made a marked impact on me and my family, as I have personally witnessed the fruit of his life and message. Anyone who desires to live a life free from fear has found his or her appointed reading. *Bulletproof* is a must-read.

Matt Gonzales
Campus pastor, evangelist, President of Kingdom Culture Ministries
www.KCMlive.org

I have known Jeff Rostocil for over two decades and have seen his life up close. During this time, one of the things that stands out about Jeff is his character and consciousness of God's right to every part of his life. He lives out what he believes and genuinely loves people the way Christ taught that we should. As Jeff has traveled and ministered and has lived out his Christian journey, Jeff is battle-tested enough to speak on the subject of "bulletproof" and has come out with a firm belief of God's providence and protection of His children and Heaven's purpose with your life. You are a weapon in God's hands that will make a strategic difference. The end-times are not happening to true believers....true believers are happening to the end-times.

Sean Smith

@RevSeanSmith, founder of Pointblank Intl

Author of *Prophetic Evangelism* and *I Am Your Sign*

www.seansmithministries.com

Like a supernatural Homeland Security director, Jeff Rostocil unveils Psalm 91 as a Top Secret document written to protect the saints from every form of enemy invasion. *Bulletproof* is an engaging account of thousands of years of God's divine protection for His people. Jeff's insights are inspiring, his stories are gripping and his research is compelling. Yet *Bulletproof* is more than a theological study or a collection of exciting stories (although it is all of that). It's a training manual, filled with a warrior's wisdom, written from a foxhole on the front lines of the battlefield of life. Jeff Rostocil teaches us how to stare down the dogs of doom, inoculate ourselves from biological attacks, avoid natural disasters, take authority over wild beasts and snakes (I hate snakes) and deal with thugs and rapists. This book is a refuge from danger, a harbor in a great storm and a beaten path to the shadow of His wings. Every believer should read this book to learn how to *Bulletproof* his or her life, loved ones and property. I guarantee that you *won't* be bored!

Kris Vallotton

Co-Founder of Bethel School of Supernatural Ministry

Author of eight books, including, *The Supernatural Ways of Royalty* and *Spirit Wars*

Leader, Bethel Church, Redding, California

Psalm 91 has been a huge encouragement to Denise and me through thirty years of ministry, propelling my vision and faith. Jeff's insight into this psalm will surely encourage you to walk in confidence and courage. Thank you, Jeff, for your insight.

Paul Goulet
Author and Lead Pastor of International Church of Las Vegas

BULLETPROOF

DESTINY IMAGE BOOKS BY JEFF ROSTOCIL

Unshakable

BULLETPROOF

ACCESSING THE FAVOR AND
PROTECTION OF GOD IN THE SECRET PLACE

JEFF ROSTOCIL

DESTINY IMAGE® PUBLISHERS, INC.

P.O. Box 310, Shippensburg, PA 17257-0310

"Promoting Inspired Lives."

This book and all other Destiny Image, Revival Press, MercyPlace, Fresh Bread, Destiny Image Fiction, and Treasure House books are available at Christian bookstores and distributors worldwide.

For a U.S. bookstore nearest you, call **1-800-722-6774.**

For more information on foreign distributors, call **717-532-3040.**

Reach us on the Internet: **www.destinyimage.com.**

ISBN 13 TP: 978-0-7684-4205-2

ISBN 13 Ebook: 978-0-7684-8742-8

For Worldwide Distribution, Printed in the U.S.A.

1 2 3 4 5 6 7 8 / 17 16 15 14 13

DEDICATION

I **DEDICATE** this book to Jane Manley, a humble and remarkable woman of God and a true mother in Israel. You have selflessly and sacrificially labored in intercession for many years and for many nations, leaders, and people. I look to you as a prayer mentor and a spiritual mother, and you are worthy of double honor. Thank you for the long hours you have spent praying for me, encouraging me, prophesying over me and imparting to me the majesty and glory of Psalm 91.

ACKNOWLEDGEMENTS

TO THE house of bread community that meets in our home, thank you for running with the vision and taking glory in the narrow road.

To my wife Meljoné, thank you for your beautiful love and sacrifice for our family. I would thank you from the bottom of my heart but for you my heart has no bottom.

To my children, thank you for the little reminders you give me each day of what is truly important in life.

Special thanks to Sean Smith, Matt Gonzales, Ronda Ranalli, our SoleQuest partners, and all those on our intercession team.

CONTENTS

PSALM 91

He who dwells in the secret place of the Most High shall abide under the shadow of the Almighty. I will say of the LORD, "He is my refuge and my fortress; my God, in Him I will trust."

Surely He shall deliver you from the snare of the fowler and from the perilous pestilence. He shall cover you with His feathers, and under His wings you shall take refuge; his truth shall be your shield and buckler. You shall not be afraid of the terror by night, nor of the arrow that flies by day, nor of the pestilence that walks in darkness, nor of the destruction that lays waste at noonday.

A thousand may fall at your side, and ten thousand at your right hand; but it shall not come near you. Only with your eyes shall you look, and see the reward of the wicked.

Because you have made the LORD, who is my refuge, even the Most High, your dwelling place, no evil shall befall you, nor shall any plague come near your dwelling; for He shall give His angels charge over you, to keep you in all your ways. In their hands they shall bear you up, lest you dash your foot against a stone. You shall tread upon the lion and the cobra, the young lion and the serpent you shall trample underfoot.

"Because he has set his love upon Me, therefore I will deliver him; I will set him on high, because he has known My name. He shall call upon Me, and I will answer him; I will be with him in trouble; I will deliver him and honor him. With long life I will satisfy him, and show him My salvation."

INTRODUCTION

WE ARE living in precarious times. The threat of famine, disease, terrorism, political unrest, biological warfare, geophysical disaster, and economic collapse has saddled many, even believers, with uncertainty. It seems that hope for a better tomorrow is becoming an endangered species. As one billboard proclaims, "The future is not what it used to be."

Scripture is not silent about what approaches. Jesus foretold that signs like these are just *the beginning of sorrows* that await the earth. Paul predicted society becoming more crude, cruel, profane, savage, slanderous, cynical, rebellious, money-hungry, self-absorbed, and pregnant with lust before the second coming of Christ. Our precarious times will progressively become more perilous as the Day of the Lord draws near.

As stewards of a fallen planet, however, we are not left without hope. Psalm 91 stands as a timeless anchor of assurance for the righteous. It has served as a marvelous and comforting promise to God's people for over four millenniums, rewarding those who thoroughly trust in the Most High. While revealing the secrets to securing the protection and favor of God, it promises deliverance from disease, famine, terrorism, and war.

For years Psalm 91 has been a source of strength for me. I have meditated on, taught on, and been comforted by its promises. Poetically, it speaks of Christ. Prophetically, however, it speaks of the age being thrust upon us. And I firmly believe that in the years to come this portion of Scripture will serve as a major and vital prayer vocabulary for the persecuted church.

This is why I am writing to you, the end-time warrior. It is precisely uncertain times like these that incite us to renegotiate the certainty of our beliefs and inspire us to cling to what we are certain of. If ever we needed a word from Heaven, it is now.

This is your moment in history. You are called to thrive, survive, and live to revive others. Let this promise become your prophetic confidence, and may it catapult you into great exploits.

CHAPTER 1

BULLETPROOF

"No evil shall befall you, nor shall any plague come near your dwelling" (Psalm 91:10).

BOOM. BOOM. Boom. Boom. Boom. Five shots. Ten seconds. A thousand questions. The blasts echoed through the canyon of our small community.

My wife clenched my arm as I leapt out of bed. We both listened as doors slammed, voices shouted and cars sped down the street.

"He's bleeding, man. He's dying! We have to get him to a hospital!" I won't easily forget the harrowing sounds I heard while crouching for cover under our bedroom window. It sounded like a mini-war being waged in our backyard.

Gunshots make an unmistakable blast. They ring differently and distinctly from fireworks, especially in the dead of sleep. This night was no exception. Our windows shook with each shot. Our hearts raced with each round. And perhaps most unnerving was that our charming little community suddenly didn't feel so charming anymore. It didn't take long for police dogs and flashing lights to fill the night air.

As a parent your first concern is always your children. After checking in on them, to my relief they were all sound asleep. To my amazement, however, so was the entire community. Within minutes, just as abruptly as it had begun it was over. The sirens were silent and the tempest subsided, and like the sea returning to form after swallowing up a ship, it was as if nothing had ever happened.

For the next few weeks the neighborhood was abuzz. Neighbors were nattering and rumors were flying. The house in question stood dark, vacant and with visible bullet holes. Pooling together the accounts from that night, the constituency of concerned neighbors pieced together what had happened.

A disgruntled homeowner held a let's-trash-the-place-going-away party for himself the night before his foreclosure. The music was loud; the guests were raucous; the kitchen appliances were snatched and hardware stripped off the walls. Some thugs showed up and a fight broke out. One young man was pistol-whipped in the melee and five shots were fired into the air.

According to the police report no one was actually shot, and the man who was beaten survived. But we sometimes forget that bullets shot up in the air do land somewhere. It's science. What goes up must come down, but where?

Not long after that night I met a neighbor who answered this question for me. One of those stray bullets came ripping through his house and whizzed five feet from his head as he sat at his computer. In fact, the bullet was still lodged into the drywall of his office. Why he left it there I haven't a clue, but when describing that night he spoke with passion and venom. His bitterness still raged as he characterized our neighborhood like it was some besieged bunker stationed helplessly in the middle of a bloody war zone. It was only one incident, but evidently one too many, as he moved his family out of the area only a few weeks later.

His story made me pause: How far was that bullet from my head? Distance-wise it was several yards, but one twitch of the wrist and hot metal comes crashing through my house. Perhaps it finds one of my walls or, even worse, my wife or one of my children.

When we bought our home in 2008 our first spiritual act was to dedicate the new property to the Lord. I insisted it be done before spending our first night in the house. After a long day of moving and unloading it wasn't until after midnight that our bed was finally put together and all the important boxes unpacked. Meljoné and I, armed with salt, wine, oil, wooden stakes, a flashlight, and a hammer, went to each of the four corners of the property to conduct a ceremony. At each station we prayed a blessing over our home and a blessing over the land. We poured salt on the soil to cleanse it, wine for the blood of Jesus, and oil to invite the activity of the Holy Spirit. In addition to the angels, our noise piqued the curiosity of one of our neighbors. I caught him peeking out his window through the blinds only to have him quickly turn off the light when I took notice.

At each corner we also drove a wooden stake into the ground to serve as a spiritual boundary marker for our property. On each stake we inscribed a different Scripture passage. One was First John 4:19, our wedding promise. Another invoked the presence of God, while the third spoke a blessing over our children. The last stake contained Psalm 91 in its entirety.

I'm convinced that a transaction took place that night in the spirit through our attempts at securing the blessings of God for our home. Perhaps those bullets were reprogrammed to change direction in mid-flight because of it. We may never know, but what is clear to me is that in Christ every arrow has its assignment. In other words, there is no such thing as a stray bullet in God's Kingdom.

91 REASONS

Psalm 91 stands as a radiant beacon of light, a powerful and prophetic word that pierces the darkness of our culture—a culture becoming more violent and doing so at breakneck speed. Gang warfare, sexual assault, and terrorist attacks dominate the media and threaten our streets. Flash mobs, carjackings, and home invasions are the darlings of copycat criminals. Predators stalk our children at Walmart. Hatred fuels the bloodshed of the Middle East. Teenage aggression entertains the masses on YouTube. Even traveling south of the border can no longer be taken for granted.

Statistics report that every nine seconds a woman is assaulted or beaten in America. Domestic violence is the leading cause of injury to women, and every day in the U.S. more than three women are murdered by their husband or boyfriend.[1]

Our children are being baptized into a culture of carnage. Violent video games are desensitizing and demoralizing a generation. It no longer shocks us when we read of babies having babies, babies raising babies and babies killing babies. Places that should be safe like the home, the school, the church, and the womb, are no longer.

The enemy resorts to brutality when he has no other recourse, and if violence doesn't terrify the faint of heart, then the threat of nuclear war, infectious disease and natural disaster will. There are ninety-one reasons to retreat and ninety-one reasons to rejoice, and standing up in the midst of the chaos as a voice of sanity is Psalm 91.

SONG OF KINGS

Psalm 91 is referred to as "The Royal Psalm." Some propose it was recited to kings before they went into battle, while others believe it was spoken by the priest as entrance liturgy to the synagogue. The Targum, an Aramaic translation of the Old Testament, suggests that is was a recorded conversation between King David and his son Solomon.[2]

Of all the psalms, Psalm 91 may be the most brilliant. It is not likely the author could have anticipated the worldwide impact these verses would make. Simon de Muis, a seventeenth-century French Hebraist, wrote, "It is one of the most excellent works of its kind which has ever appeared. It is impossible to imagine anything more solid, more beautiful, more profound or more ornamented…we have no poem, either in Greek or Latin, comparable to this Hebrew ode."[3]

Liturgical in style, this poem is as useful as it is beautiful. Incorporating frequent voice changes, some suppose it was to be sung by a choir with alternative responses. Voice #1 is introduced in verse 1 and returns in verses 3-8 and 9b-13. Voice #2 speaks up in verse 2 and again in verse 9a. The song closes with Voice #3, the Most High Himself, who is evidently addressing the angels.

Though some scholars attribute it to David or Moses, its authorship is largely unknown. What is evident, however, is that it was written by someone possessing a deep history with God.

RUNNING FOR COVER

The story of Psalm 91 is not too different from the story of the three little pigs. In the famed nursery rhyme the big bad wolf comes to the first pig whose house is made of hay. The wolf huffs and puffs and blows his house down. He comes to the second pig's house made of sticks. He huffs and puffs and blows his house down as well. But when the wolf comes to the house made of bricks, he could not blow it down. It was bulletproof, or in this case, hurricane retrofitted.

"The house of the righteous will stand" (Proverbs 12:7b).

The brick house can be likened to the dwelling place of Psalm 91. When we make the Lord our strong tower, the storms of life will not flatten us because we have built our lives, our marriages, our families, and our businesses on Solid Rock. Even when the devil hunts us down, breathing accusations and threatening to devour us, we will have no cause for fear. We and our households will be safe and will stand as a testimony for those around us.

There's a moral to the story of the three little pigs: Running to the wrong refuge is like trusting a chair with a broken leg. It is as foolish as it is futile, for no fortress on earth is foolproof. Riches are shaky and friends can be flakey; beauty fades and youth fails; fame is fickle and pleasure is unfulfilling. Deadbolts can't lock out disease, just as money can't guarantee us more revolutions around the sun. Only a Rock that is higher than us can elevate our souls when an enemy comes in like a flood.

The question we must ask ourselves is this: Where do I run to for refuge? We can learn where *not* to run and what *not* to do from the pig who abandoned his toppled house of hay for his friend's house of sticks. That's like running from one toxic relationship to another hoping for a different outcome. The answer for this pig was not another hit, high, binge, comfort meal, or financial windfall. A failed refuge has a way of leaving us soul-searching, and the house of the Most High is always at the end of that journey.

Jesus said, "Whoever falls on this stone will be broken; but on whomever it falls, it will grind him to powder" (Matt. 21:44). All will be broken, voluntarily or involuntarily, but not all need to be crushed. When life topples over on top of us, our choice is to either go belly up or get on our face; to either give up or get up humbled. There's no way around it. It will take brokenness if we want to attain a higher place with the Most High.

ESCAPE ARTISTS

Psalm 91 is not a stress-free, care-free guarantee. Neither does it address why bad things happen to good people. Look carefully. Snares, serpents, terror, trouble, arrows, plagues, pestilence, disease, danger, destruction, and evil surround the righteous just as they do the wicked. The difference, however, is not in the method but in the outcome. The pure-hearted escape what the corrupt cannot.

> Running to the wrong refuge is like trusting a chair with a broken leg.

Noah found grace in the eyes of the Lord and escaped the flood. Joseph prospered in the midst of a planet-wide famine. Moses and the children of Israel were spared the loss of their firstborn when the angel of death passed over them. Rahab's household stood while the walls of Jericho collapsed around them. All faced disaster and all were preserved in the midst of it, yet God's protection was not automatic. Each were given specific instructions that, when heeded, led to their deliverance. Noah built a boat. Joseph started a business. The Israelites painted blood over their doors. Rahab hung a scarlet cord from her window.

For us it is no different. We all will eventually face some kind of disaster and will have to decide for ourselves whether to demonstrate our trust in the Savior by carrying out His instructions. It is presumptuous, perhaps even ignorant, to assume that His protection is *carte blanche* and without condition. Just because a person attends church or is spiritually gifted doesn't mean he has secured the favor and blessings of God. What I have learned is that God will test my faith by giving me an assignment, and as I'm faithful to that assignment I find a place of refuge in His pleasure.

This happened once when I was hurrying to catch a flight out of Oakland International Airport. I had just parked my car in the long-term lot, and while walking toward the terminal, the Holy Spirit whispered, "You left your car unlocked. Go back and check it."

Thinking it was my own thoughts, I brushed it off. "I always lock my door," I reasoned. "There's no chance my car is unlocked."

The voice came again, "It is unlocked. Go back."

I did go back but admittedly only to put my worries to rest. Sure enough, the doors were unlocked. God graciously had the protection of my stereo in mind.

He could have stationed angels unbeknownst to me to guard and protect my car from burglary while I was away. He could have made it virtually invisible to thieves or appear as if the door was locked, but instead He gave me a nudge and an assignment. It was a test of my faith and an opportunity to use my cooperation as an ingredient to His work.

I must admit it doesn't always turn out this way for me. There are countless occasions when I've ignored His leadings to my own regret. Sometimes it is His desire that we endure hardships like a good soldier of Christ. At other times He protects us without our knowledge. But it is those divine moments when we've successfully discerned the thoughts of Heaven that we get a foretaste of what is accessible to us that perhaps we've been neglecting.

There is a higher plane available to those who walk with the Most High, a place where worldly worries, sinful consequences, and the wrath of God do not befall us. The pure are never designed to be swept away in the same flood of judgment as the profane, for it is a holy thing to God that His saints are not judged alongside sinners. This is why there are two judgments at the end of the age—the Great White Throne and the Bema Seat. One is for the sheep, the other for the goats.

Tragedy may strike, but it's our reaction to it that separates us from the godless. What throws the world into a tailspin of anger, bitterness, and suicide should not break us. While they consult the stars, we consult the One who created them. While they seek the hands of doctors, we seek the hand of the Great Physician. When they get stressed out, we have a peace that passes understanding. It is precisely our response to sin, sickness, rejection, persecution, financial problems, and death that makes us bulletproof.

LONGEVITY

This is not to say that believers who die at a young age or in tragic accidents strayed from the will of God. The answers to life and death are not that simple. Our confidence, however, is that when we keep in step with the heartbeat of Heaven, our lives will not be shortened one second sooner than the sovereign timing of our Maker.

> *"With long life I will satisfy him, and show him My salvation"*
> (Psalm 91:16).

Longevity is the reward of the refugee. Those who trust in the Lord are delivered from the vices that seek to deprive them of the vigor of life. Because they find contentment and joy in the presence of the Living God, they are able to navigate the pitfalls of life and outlive the ungodly. In this sense, long life is more of a choice we make than a random occurrence. We choose how long we live by how we live. We are already promised long life as our inheritance, but it is our choice whether to access it or not.

The exception, of course, is martyrdom. There is perhaps no greater honor in Heaven or on earth than to be found worthy to take a bullet for the Kingdom. What martyrs lose here on earth is more than gained in eternity, so that even death cannot take away God's promises from them. While you can put a bullet in their body, you cannot make a dent in their spirit. Whether or not you and I are martyred, we can be confident that when we place our trust in the Most High, the testimony of our lives is scripted by heaven.

The point of Psalm 91 is that those who preserve their purity in times of widespread corruption will be kept safe in times of widespread destruction. Our assurance is not a life without problems but a life immune from the poison of those problems.

SPIRITUAL IMMUNITY

Our immune systems are remarkably complex and wonderfully organized. They're like a germ-fighting, pathogen-destroying SWAT team embedded right into our bodies. They employ a multi-layered system of defense that effectively recognizes, resists and eradicates harmful intruders like infection, bacteria, parasites, viruses, and tumor cells.

Innate immunity is the outer layer of our immune system's defense and is the body's first line of resistance. It serves as a general barrier to hinder the entrance and spread of disease. Adaptive immunity is the inner layer. It tailors a targeted, smart defense by launching a specific attack against a foreign invader.[4]

Psalm 91 is our promise of a storybook ending.

Healthy immune systems can easily locate and destroy harmful agents. The average person, for example, develops a couple cancer cells at least two hundred times in their lifetime. Properly functioning cells naturally resist cancer cells, and when the immune system is strong our cells will never become cancerous. An immune system that is compromised, however, does not recognize when it is under attack. This is when the body becomes more susceptible to disease.[5]

Immunity engenders liberty. To be immune means to be free—free from communicable agents, destructive intruders, and unwanted trespassers. Due to the presence of antibodies an immune person is no longer susceptible to a threatening disease or infection.[6]

Psalm 91 is our promise of freedom and immunity. We have a demon-fighting, evil-resisting SWAT team embedded right into our souls. Dwelling in the secret place builds up our immunity, liberates us from destructive forces, and alerts our spirits to attack. Since immunity involves the body's power to resist, progress in the spirit requires aggressive action as well. You will have to fight for your marriage, your ministry, your anointing, your health, your children, and your spiritual inheritance. There is no off-season in this war, and there is no place for passivity.

UNITY & IMMUNITY

Once while meditating on these verses, I felt the Lord impress this upon me: *There will never be complete immunity until there is complete unity.* I believe this applies in two ways.

First, our immunity in this world hinges on our unity with Christ. We've got to fight for nothing short of the fullness of God in our personal walk with Him. This is where true freedom is attained. Only in Christ are we free to make wise decisions, free to want what we need and to not need what our flesh wants. Abiding teaches us how avoid the pitfalls that the world falls into and how to guard ourselves from being overtaken by physical, emotional, or personal turmoil.

Second, our disunity in the body of Christ may be exposing us to excessive warfare. Satan knows that if he can keep us divided, confused, and busy attacking each other, we will have no strength to resist him. Eventually it will decimate our numbers.

This is how autoimmune diseases operate. With this disorder, the immune system gets thrown into a state of confusion. The corpuscles think that the body is the enemy and attack it. Instead of protecting the body, they destroy it.

I know of several churches that are plagued with an autoimmune disease. Their backbiting, gossip, slander, control, unrighteous judgment, and power struggles are cancerous and are tearing them apart. They've proverbially turned the gun on themselves and made it an all-out civil war. The same could be said for some families as well. If Satan can keep us confused and fighting each other, we may never stand up to the real threat he poses.

Our immunity, both physical and spiritual, is tied to our unity in Christ and with each other. It has been documented that when a person's heart is severely broken and damaged by another, his immune system gets destabilized and weakened. Heartache, bitterness, sin, and the betrayal of others cause our immune systems to be compromised. Studies have shown, however, that laughter works the opposite way—it strengthens the immune system by stimulating the body to manufacture T cells and killer cells.[7] So then, if sin removes us from the protection of God's covering, finding joy in each other must play a role in restoring it.

LINE OF FIRE

Several months after the shooting incident we were having problems with water draining off our roof properly. A roofer came by to do an inspection, and when I asked him to be on the lookout for any kind of bullet markings, he told me a story. While doing some work on a nearby house, he found a .38 slug lodged into one of the roof tiles. Thankfully, upon his inspection, there was no evidence of bullet holes in our roof. Our home had proven to be out of the line of fire, but the question still lingered: Why ours and not someone else's? One neighbor has a lethal projectile come zipping past his ear while another sleeps soundly. One family is vulnerable. The other is bulletproof.

> *"No evil shall befall you, nor shall any plague come near your dwelling"* (Psalm 91:10).

The book of Proverbs draws a stark contrast between the house of the righteous and the house of the wicked.

> *"The curse of the LORD is on the house of the wicked, but He blesses the home of the just"* (Proverbs 3:33).

"The wicked are overthrown and are no more, but the house of the righteous will stand" (Proverbs 12:7).

"The house of the wicked will be overthrown, but the tent of the upright will flourish" (Proverbs 14:11).

"In the house of the righteous there is much treasure, but in the revenue of the wicked is trouble" (Proverbs 15:6).

"The righteous God wisely considers the house of the wicked, overthrowing the wicked for their wickedness" (Proverbs 21:12).

The house of the righteous is full of treasure, blessed, flourishing, and enduring. Conversely, the house of the wicked is troubled, cursed, overthrown, and perishing. Psalm 91 assures us that the fate of the ungodly does not have to be ours. Righteousness is still the industry leader in home security.

THE BULLET POINT

Is your refuge bulletproof? Spiritual covering is beneficial, but are you relying on an earthly covering to accomplish what only a heavenly covering can provide? The Most High is the highest spiritual covering we can secure, and Psalm 91 compels us to trust in a God who is all-together trustworthy. Hope in Him, run to His refuge, and embrace brokenness. It's through faith and fortitude that we inherit the promises of God and the fortunes of Psalm 91.

The remainder of this book unpacks Psalm 91 verse by verse, outlining its benefits and how to access its rewards. Although the majority of our lives are not lived in threatening danger, that may not be a luxury the end-time church enjoys. That's all the more reason this ancient psalm carries relevance and significance. As we move forward may you be fully prepared for what lies ahead. May these words equip you to remain in the Spirit in times of crisis and catapult you into fearless living.

ENDNOTES

1. "Domestic Violence Statistics," accessed August 5, 2012, http://domesticviolencestatistics.org/domestic-violence-statistics/.

2. Adam Clarke, *Clarke's Commentary* (Electronic Database, Biblesoft, 1997), Psalm 91.

3. Ibid.

4. Encarta Encyclopedia 2000, Microsoft Corporation, 1993–1999.

5. Henry Wright, *A More Excellent Way* (Thomaston, GA: Pleasant Valley Publications, 1999), 122, 138.

6. *Webster's New World Dictionary* (New York, NY: Prentice Hall Press, 1986), s.v. "immune."

7. Wright, *A More Excellent Way*, 62.

CHAPTER 2

THE SECRET PLACE

*"He who **dwells in the secret place** of the Most High shall abide under the shadow of the Almighty"* (Psalm 91:1).

PSALM 91 is a summons to the secret place, a sacred and holy invitation to pursue the mysteries of the Most High. Not everyone will answer this call, not even every believer. Many are unaware of it; few ever access it; even fewer dwell there.

Jesus spoke of a secret place in His sermon on the mount. "When you pray, go into your room, and when you have shut your door, pray to your Father who is in the secret place; and your Father who sees in secret will reward you openly" (Matt. 6:6). About fasting He repeats, "Your Father who is in the secret place… will reward you openly" (Matt. 6:18b).

Of all our Kingdom pursuits there is no substitute for prayer and fasting. Church meetings and Christian service have their place, but they cannot replace time spent seeking His face. These divine moments have been enjoyed by men and women since the beginning of time and are meant to be regular, personal, and unique to the life of every believer.

Andrew Murray writes, "Fasting helps to express, to deepen and to confirm the resolution that we are ready to sacrifice ourselves to attain what we seek for the kingdom. Prayer is the one hand with which we grasp the Invisible; fasting is the other with which we let loose and cast away the visible."[1]

The secret place of the Most High is a force to be reckoned with. Influence gained here is the highest law of the universe, having the ability to suspend all other laws of science by sanctioning divine intervention. The secret place comes not to the casual or the hasty. Neither can we be taught or brought into it by education or human ingenuity. It is entered privately and alone. To find it the Holy One must become our escort and our companion. Once found, no person can restrain us; no evil can remove us.

Note that the promises of the secret place are neither universal nor exclusive but conditional, reserved for the "one who dwells in the secret place" (v.1). Only the person abiding in the secret place, having made the Lord his or her resting place, can claim the assurances of this psalm. It is this premise that qualifies one for the promises of these verses. God's protection is not automatically ours just because we're Christians, and we cannot blame God if we are not experiencing the full blessing of Psalm 91. It is an indication that we have not yet established ourselves in the secret place.

Charles Spurgeon preached eloquently, "It is not every professing Christian, nor every believer who attains this height of experience; but only such as believe the promise, and fulfill the heavenly condition of dwelling in the secret place of the Most High. How could cholera and fever get into the secret place of the Most High? How could arrows, how could pestilence, ever be able to reach that secure abode of God? If you dwell there, you are invincible, invulnerable, infinitely secure."[2]

> Once you find the secret place, no one can restrain you and no evil can remove you.

SECRET PLACE SECRETS

Every believer needs a God-cave, a foxhole, a place he can run to and bare his soul before his Creator. It should be a place where no one else is welcome, not even a spouse. The secret place of the Most High is this place. It is your divine stakeout, your place in the presence of God. You were created for it, and it was created for you. It is your sanctuary.

For Moses, it was the holy of holies, the place where the glory of God rested. For David, it was the pavilion, a hidden fortress, the central tent of his Commanding Officer.[3] For Elijah, it was the mountain of God; and for us, it is Christ, the One in whom all these consist.

God's throne room is also God's laundry room. In His presence all is exposed, all is laid bare, all is cleansed. Here we exchange weakness for strength, poison for honey and soiled garments for robes of righteousness. Smith Wigglesworth said, "There is no kick in the secret place—no evil temper, no irritability. All is swept away while one is dwelling in the presence of the Almighty; in the covering of God."[4]

I have found that the rewards of the secret place are numerous and plentiful but not always immediate. Times of concentrated prayer, fasting, and worship are often seed-sowing investments of time. Although I may not see immediate change and instant fruit on my efforts, I am sowing into a harvest of future returns.

When Jesus said, "Your Father who sees in secret will reward you openly" (Matt. 6:6, 18), He is making a connection between our private life and our public life, affirming that our outer history can be shaped and written by our inner history with God. The secret place then becomes a training place for the marketplace. Times of direct focus serve to heighten our general awareness and prepare us to face the world, while purifying and even multiplying our time.

The secret place is a supernatural place of empowerment like no other. Consistent and lasting spiritual victory on the battleground is linked to consistent and considerable attention given to the holy ground. I have observed that my confidence and precision in the spirit are directly related to time spent in the prayer closet.

THE BIG O

Another definition should be considered when seeking to live in the secret place. The Hebrew word for "secret place" is *cether*. Elsewhere it is translated *hiding place, covering* or *secrecy*. "You are my *hiding place*; you shall preserve me from trouble…" (Ps. 32:7). "You are my *hiding place* and my shield; I hope in Your word" (Ps. 119:114).

Its root is *cathar*, meaning *hidden* or *concealed*.

> *"The secret things [cether] belong to the LORD our God, but those things which are revealed belong to us and to our children forever, that we may do all the words of this law"* (Deuteronomy 29:29).

> *"Seek the LORD, all you meek of the earth, who have upheld His justice. Seek righteousness, seek humility. It may be that you will be hidden [cether] in the day of the LORD's anger"* (Zephaniah 2:3).

> *"For in the time of trouble He shall hide me in His pavilion; in the secret place [cether] of His tabernacle He shall hide me [cathar]"* (Psalm 27:5).

> *"Oh, how great is Your goodness, which You have laid up for those who fear You, which You have prepared for those who trust in You in the presence of the sons of men! You shall hide them [cathar] in the secret place of [cether] Your presence from the plots of man; You shall keep them secretly in a pavilion from the strife of tongues"* (Psalm 31:19-20).

The secret place is a hidden life of surrender, a brand of living that secures for us protection against the forces of darkness. It is more than an event or quiet time—it is a consecrated life. Much like Psalm 83:3 speaks of the "sheltered ones," God Himself becomes a shelter for those who embrace the fear of the Lord. Humility, justice, faithfulness, and obedience mark those who walk this path of consecration.

Obedience is a secret place. The Father delights to dwell with the obedient, and He crowns them with His love and favor. Only one thing was asked of Adam in the garden. "The LORD God commanded the man, saying…" (Gen. 2:16). Obedience was the virtue than governed the garden, the one condition to Adam remaining and dwelling there. There is no mention of faith or love or humility because obedience covers them all.

In the last chapter of Revelation, John writes, "Blessed are those who do His commandments, that they may have the right to the tree of life…" (Rev. 22:14). So we see that from paradise lost to paradise regained, from start to finish, from beginning to end the theme of Scripture is consistent. Obedience to God's commands is the gateway to gaining the applause of Heaven and eating of the tree of life. It is the one virtue that governs the secret place.[5]

Noah knew a thing or two about God's deliverance. He also knew a thing or two about obedience. More than once Scripture reads that Noah "did according to all that the Lord commanded him." His life prophesies to us that although the price of obedience may be high, the price of disobedience can be deadly.

DEADLY TEMPTATIONS

Once, when I was living in Chico, I was running late to a speaking engagement. The drive to the church was over an hour, so I admit I was pushing the speed limit a bit. I decided to take a less-traveled back road to get to the highway faster. Racing down the two-lane road, I approached a railroad crossing at a blind intersection. The train tracks were hidden by rows of tress, making it difficult to see how close or far away an approaching train could be. As I sped toward the crossing, the warning lights flashed and the gates dropped in front of me. It was too late. I had missed beating it by just a few seconds.

My experience on these back roads was that the railroad guards usually drop a good minute in advance of a ridiculously long ninety-five-car freight train that seems to chug way too slow and take way too long. I considered this an unwanted and ill-afforded interruption to my schedule. I had thoughts of just keeping up my speed, swerving in between the gates and darting over the tracks. I figured I could do it in about two seconds tops. Being in a hurry and with no other cars around, I was tempted, but then I heard an internal voice say, "Be wise, Jeff. Obey the law."

By the grace of God I listened and stopped. It was not more than a moment or two later that a speeding locomotive raced through the railroad crossing at top speed. Had I foolishly broken the law and not heeded the warning, my car would have served as my casket.

That day I learned a valuable lesson. My impatience and disregard for traffic laws almost cost me my life. Graciously the Holy Spirit alerted my spirit and thankfully I listened.

Heeding God's voice and walking in wisdom are not always the most comfortable or the most popular courses of action. Humbling ourselves, biting our tongue, preferring others, honoring our word, upholding our convictions, being honest, patient, and loyal can be an inconvenient and sometimes bitter pill to swallow; but it can also be joyous when our heart is set upon loving God. Although there is a price to pay for obedience, there is also a privilege—the privilege of pleasing our Father.

A FATHER'S REQUEST

In the story of the two sons, Jesus narrates how to please the heavenly Father while illustrating the superiority and importance of deeds over creeds. Two sons are asked by their father to work the day in the vineyard. The first one answers, "I will not" but relents and works. The second son initially agrees to work but never gets around to it. Then Jesus asks, "Which one did the will of his father?" The answer is obvious.

Saying "Yes" to God the Father means nothing if our prayer is not reinforced with dutiful and faithful obedience. Our prayers may be full of good intentions and great faith, but it is our obedience that justifies us before the Father.

Prayer is not the only secret place.

Obedience is the secret to pleasing the heart of the Father and finding protection from the consequences that overtake the rebellious. It was disobedience that shut us off from God's presence in the first place, and it's obedience that opens it back up. This obedience is not ours, but Christ's. "By the obedience of one shall many be made righteous" (Rom. 5:19b KJV). Jesus is the tree of life, and it is His aim to restore life and obedience to Adam's race.

Although prayer is a secret place, it cannot be the only secret place that Psalm 91 speaks of. Excluding obedience from the secret place only limits the potency and glory of it. Perhaps we haven't given obedience its proper place in our abiding. Prayer, worship, and soaking are important, but it is through consecration with obedience that we sustain God's presence and favor long term. If Psalm 91 shows us anything, it's that a life of continuous obedience is possible.

Some of the best insights on life in the secret place can be found within the psalm itself.

1. Keep the secret place personal.

"I will say of the LORD, 'He is my refuge and my fortress; my God, in Him I will trust'" (Psalm 91:2).

In the secret place we learn to trust our Shepherd and obey Him on a personal level. He is not just anyone and everyone's shelter, but He is *"my* refuge," *"my* fortress," and *"my* God." Here, we exchange an academic knowledge of the Most High for an experiential one.

The Creator of the universe wants to be intimately involved and included in every activity of our lives, and it is our privilege to invite Him into our thoughts, homes, and decisions. Just because He is all-knowing doesn't mean He acts like a know-it-all or doesn't care about interacting with us. Invite Him into your disappointments, challenges, victories, opportunities, and defeats. Cry with Him, laugh with Him, grieve with Him, be with Him. It won't take long before He becomes your first choice and not your last resort.

2. Stay undercover.

"He shall cover you with His feathers, and under His wings you shall take refuge..." (Psalm 91:4).

Some things are too sacred for public scrutiny. The marriage bed, for example, is a private matter between a husband and wife. It should remain undercover or, shall we say, under the covers.

The secret place is similar. It is our duty to keep the secret place a secret from those who wish to disrupt it. Too often we swing wide the door of our private God-life to any onlooker or floating thought that passes by. We would do well to guard our intimacy with Him. When we drag the world and its pursuits into our prayer times, it compromises the hiddenness of that place, threatening to jeopardize and un-secretize the trust we have built with the Father.

3. Awaken love.

"Because he has set his love upon Me, therefore I will deliver him" (Psalm 91:14a).

This phrase "because he has set his love upon Me" can also be translated "because he longs for Me" or "because he has become attached to Me."[6] In other words, God uses the secret place to thrill us and awaken our fascination, to captivate us and draw out our passions. As we direct our affections toward our heavenly Lover, we find ourselves becoming the main character in the greatest love story of all time. Our life with Him then is a living, written romance novel, and the secret place is where our story is chronicled.

4. Resort to name calling.

"I will set him on high, because he has known My name" (Psalm 91:14b).

In Hebrew culture knowing God's name is nearly equivalent to knowing Him. Perhaps this is why in the first two verses alone the writer of Psalm 91 uses four different names for God: *Elyon,* "The Most High" (vv. 1, 9); *El Shaddai,* "The Almighty" (v. 1); *Yehovah,* "The Lord" (vv. 2, 9); and *Elohim,* "My God" (v. 2).

Like a master artist the psalmist paints a brilliant portrait of a supremely powerful God who is surprisingly personal. He is both great in power and good in heart. He is the Most High, elevated above all our circumstances. He is the Almighty, stronger than any force on earth. He is Yehovah, the One who has revealed Himself to us, and He is my God, in whom I trust.

Finding new names for the ones we love is a common expression of love. We call them terms of endearment, and this is exactly what happens when we follow our Maker into the secret place. Our romance with Him becomes multi-faceted as we take on His nature and His name. The more time we spend seeking Him and His ways, the more we recognize Him and the more He recognizes us. He becomes our Deliverer, our Protector and our Confidence. We look to Him, for He is our *El Elyon.* We marvel at His works, for He is our *El Shaddai.* We learn from His ways, for His name is *Yehovah,* and we take Him as our own, for He is our *Elohim.*

5. Pull an audible.

"He shall call upon Me, and I will answer him…" (Psalm 91:15).

The greatest motivation for prayer is, no surprise here, answered prayer. When God begins to consistently and promptly answer your prayers, you can know that your heart and His will have been synchronized. When this happens it is as natural for God to answer as it is for us to ask.

The beauty of the secret place is that it both motivates us to pray and liberates us from the guilt of not praying enough. We would be hard-pressed to find a believer who feels he or she prays sufficiently. Be relieved to know that any condemnation concerning your prayer life is unnecessary, ungodly, and counterproductive to the work of intercession. We all go through ups and downs in the discipline of prayer. You are not alone. Thankfully, your struggle to give prayer its proper attention does not need to affect your life of love and good works. When your energy for prayer is low, your consecration keeps you hidden in Him.

THE BULLET POINT

The secret place is an untapped gold mine stockpiled with treasures beyond our wildest imagination. We have yet to exhaust the riches of this place. Of its fortunes, none is more precious than constant, consistent, and continual interaction with the Holy One. The key to this grace is heartfelt obedience, the first and last thing God asks of us.

The psalmist writes, "I will say of the LORD," meaning that those who encamp their souls next to the Living God cannot shut up about His goodness. This kind of believer is armed with an undeniable testimony and a history that boasts of redemption's story.

God is preparing a new breed of revolutionaries forged in the fires of the secret place. Labor to find that blessed position, for there is no safety in the outer courts.

ENDNOTES

1. Andrew Murray, *With Christ in the School of Prayer* (Westwood, NJ: Fleming H. Revell Company), 98.

2. Charles H. Spurgeon, *Surgeon's Encyclopedia of Sermons*, sermon entitled: *Exposition of Psalm 91.*

3. In those days if an enemy sought to threaten the general, he would have to break through the ranks of the army to get to this well-guarded tent called the pavilion. See Psalm 27:5; 31:20.

4. "The Secret Place," Smith Wigglesworth Sermon, accessed August 6, 2012, http://wigglesworth.born-again-christian.info/smith.wigglesworth.sermons.3.htm.

5. I am indebted to the writings of Andrew Murray for these thoughts, and I highly recommend his book *The Believer's Secret of Obedience.*

6. Francis Brown, S. Driver, and C. Briggs, *BibleSoft's Brown, Driver and Briggs' Hebrew Lexicon* (Ontario, Canada: Woodside Bible Fellowship, 1993), s.v. "because he has set his love upon Me."

CHAPTER 3

SHADOW OF THE ALMIGHTY

*"He who dwells in the secret place of the Most High shall abide under the **shadow of the Almighty**"* (Psalm 91:1).

THE CONCEPT of God having a shadow is hard to grasp. Think about it. How can pure Light possess a shadow? John writes that "God is light and in Him is no darkness at all" (1 John 1:5b). James describes Him as the "Father of lights, with whom there is no variation or shadow of turning" (James 1:17b).

Shadows are formed when an object eclipses light. A light source contains no shadow in itself really. It merely produces a shadow for something else. The light only casts a shadow when there is something to stand in its way.

When we see our shadows on a sunny day, for example, the shadow appears due to the position of our physical body in relation to the sun. Our body eclipses the sun and a silhouette is formed of our image. Likewise, a light bulb must employ a shade or a wall to produce a shadow. A shadow, then, is cast by an object shading a light source. This begs the question: If God is the Source of all light, how then can He shadow Himself?

45

When we think of shadows, we often envision dark shades, vague outlines, and faint silhouettes. We describe obscure figures as *shadowy* and sinister characters as *shady*. Is this what the psalmist means?

It helps to think in spiritual terms. A spiritual shadow behaves differently than a physical one. A physical shadow eclipses light and produces darkness, but a spiritual shadow eclipses darkness and shines forth revelation. An earthly shadow is a dark figure, but a heavenly shadow is a collection

> A spiritual shadow eclipses darkness and shines forth revelation.

and reflection of divine glory. A human shadow is an outline of our image; a divine shadow is an extension of God's image. Our shadows block light; His reveals it. What I've come to realize is that God's shadow is not dark at all. It is full of radiant light just as He is! This light protects, refreshes, illuminates, and rejuvenates all who rest under it.

UNDER THE FIG TREE

Hebrew writers often employ a style of poetry called parallelism, where an individual verse contains two or more components forming an internal parallel relationship. Often the two thoughts are synonymous—the second line of the verse repeats and rewords the thought expressed in the first line. Presumably this is done for emphasis and clarity.[1]

Psalm 91 is full of parallelisms, and verse 1 is no exception.

> *"He who dwells in the secret place of the Most High shall abide under the shadow of the Almighty"* (Psalm 91:1).

Using this style of poetry, abiding under the shadow of the Almighty is parallel to dwelling in the secret place. The writer uses figurative language here to illustrate a spiritual truth. Dwelling in the secret place is like resting under the shade of a tree, maybe even the shade of a fig tree.

In Hebrew language resting "under the fig tree" is an idiom used for finding a place of meditation. It refers to one's home or garden where study and solitude take place.[2] When Jesus said to Nathanael, "I saw you under the fig tree" (John 1:50), He wasn't speaking of a physical tree as much as He was referencing Nathanael's place of solitude.[3]

> *"Jesus saw Nathanael coming toward Him, and said of him, 'Behold, an Israelite indeed, in whom is no deceit!' Nathanael said to Him, 'How do You know me?' Jesus answered and said to him, 'Before Philip called you, when you were under the fig tree, I saw you.' Nathanael answered and said to Him, 'Rabbi, You are the Son of God! You are the King of Israel!' Jesus answered and said to him, 'Because I said to you, "I saw you under the fig tree," do you believe? You will see greater things than these.' And He said to him, 'Most assuredly, I say to you, hereafter you shall see heaven open, and the angels of God ascending and descending upon the Son of Man'"* (John 1:47-51).

Jesus had prophetic insight about the meditation of Nathanael's heart. It may be that Nathanael was sitting *under his fig tree* meditating on the life of Jacob when Philip found him. Perhaps he was even hoping that if the Holy One of Israel would reveal Himself to a deceitful man such as Jacob, He might reveal Himself to Nathanael. Philip then interrupts him telling him that they have found the One sent from above!

This scenario might help explain why Jesus used the phrase "Israelite in whom is no deceit" to describe Nathanael. Jacob's name means deceiver, and Israel is the new name the angel gave to Jacob. The fact that Jesus references the life of Jacob upon their first meeting was a sign given to Nathanael that Jesus of Nazareth was the subject of his meditation and very answer to his prayer.

Nathanael says, "Rabbi, You are the Son of God! You are the King of Israel!" What would warrant such a thunderous response? Nathanael makes the connection between the Master's greeting and his recent place of study. He realizes that Jesus had been *resting in the secret place* with him and is now even revealing the very desires and secrets of his heart. This explains why Nathanael makes such a bold proclamation of Jesus' identity.

Not to allow His disciples to be too impressed by His word of knowledge, Jesus promises that they will see even greater things than Jacob did. "You shall see heaven open, and the angels of God ascending and descending upon the Son of Man." Jesus declares Himself to be the revelation and fulfillment of Jacob's ladder.

SHADOW OF THE FATHER

One of the great wonders of Psalm 91 is that it is Messianic, meaning that it prophesies the life and identity of the Anointed One. It was no mistake that Satan quoted from this psalm to tempt Jesus in the desert. Psalm 91 is about the Messiah. Jesus is the Fearless One who dwells in the secret place and abides under the shadow of the Almighty. He is the One who loves the Father, takes refuge in Him and is full of truth. Satan and the Son of God both knew to whom, for whom and about whom this psalm was written.

But there's more. Jesus is not just the subject of this promise. He is also the manifestation of it. The Shadow of the Almighty is as much a Person as it is a position. Someone must be standing in the way of El Shaddai in order to produce a shadow, and that someone is the Son of God. The Father shadowed Himself in His Son.

Christ *is* the Shadow of the Almighty. He came to earth as the Shade at God's Right Hand and a Shelter for the weary. Isaiah titled Him the Shadow of God's Hand.[4] He is the revelation and the representation of the Father, the extension of His image, the "express image of His person" (Heb. 1:3). While on earth He stood in all of God's ways and was the reflection of His being, and at His appearing all darkness must flee. Jesus is both the One who abides in the secret place and the secret place we abide in!

ABIDING IN THE VINE

The parallels drawn between John 15 and Psalm 91 are undeniable.

Psalm 91	John 15
"He who dwells…shall abide" (v. 1)	"Abide in Me, and I in you" (v. 4)
"Because he has set his love upon Me" (v. 14a)	"As the Father has loved Me, I also have loved you; abide in My love" (v. 9)
"Because he has known my Name" (v. 14b)	"Ask the Father in My name" (v. 16)
"Call upon Me, and I will answer" (v. 15)	"Ask what you desire, and it shall be done for you" (v. 7)

When Jesus said, "Abide in Me, and I in you" (John 15:4), He became our Refuge. When He said, "As the Father loved Me, I also have loved you" (John 15:9), He became our Lover. When He said, "Whatever you ask the Father in my name" (John 15:16), He became the Name by which we access Heaven. When He said, "I have called you friends" (John 15:15), He became the One who sticks closer than a brother.

Francis Frangipane writes, "Our primary purpose in life must be to abide in Christ. Otherwise we can become so consumed with the deteriorating condition of the world that we fail to see the deteriorating condition of our own soul."[5]

Andrew Murray adds, "How often and how earnestly we have asked the way to abide continually in Christ! We have thought more

> Jesus is both the One who abides in the secret place and the secret place we abide in.

49

study of the Word, more faith, more prayer, more communion with God, but we have overlooked a simple truth. Jesus teaches so clearly, 'If you keep my commandments, you shall abide in my love'…the only way under heaven to abide in the divine love is to keep the commandments.'[6]

Friendship with God is not bestowed upon everyone. Jesus said, "You are My friends if you do whatever I command you" (John 15:14). Certainly all who have repented have fallen into the arms of a friendly God, but friendship with the Holy One is reserved for those who walk in the light as He is in the light. Abraham was called the friend of God after his act of faith, not before.[7] A profession of faith does not automatically secure friendship with the Almighty. This kind of relationship is only gained through time, trust, and consistent surrender.

OVERSHADOWED BY GOD

Peter is one of the major characters of the New Testament. He went from being a fisherman to a fisher of men; from a reed to a rock. He walked through great failure but also walked on water. Called, commissioned, renamed, rebuked, restored, and loved, this great apostle seemed to shadow Jesus wherever He went.

To shadow someone means to trail another, to closely follow his every move. Peter is not the only one in Scripture to have shadowed the Shepherd of Israel. Enoch walked with Elohim and was no more. Moses talked to Him face to face. Elijah was caught up to Heaven in a whirlwind.

In Acts 5, the tables get turned on Peter. The Holy Spirit overshadows him! The result was a man who was once practically afraid of his own shadow now possessing the most lethal shadow in the Middle East. Peter's shadow could heal disease and terrify demons. It was a supernatural, miracle-working, disease-crushing, demon-busting, life-giving shadow that contained the same ingredients of the shadow of the Almighty—healing and deliverance.

The word "overshadow" here means *to envelop in a haze of brilliancy*.[8] Is it possible that Peter so discovered the secret of abiding in Christ, living under the shadow of the Almighty, that the Holy Spirit chose to shadow him and his shadow? Enveloped in a haze of brilliancy, Peter and his shadow became an extension and expression of God's healing and delivering power.

This is not the first time this kind of event occurs in Scripture. In the account of creation, the Spirit of God *overshadowed* the face of the waters when it was without form and void.[9] The Holy Spirit *overshadowed* Mary when she was impregnated with the Christ child.[10] Peter, James and John were *enveloped in a haze of brilliancy* when Jesus transfigured right before their eyes on the mountain in a cloud of glory.[11]

Significant things happen when the Holy Spirit overshadows: sickness retreats, demons recoil, creation is born, life is conceived, Heaven speaks audibly, the glory of God comes, and Moses and Elijah make an appearance. Now that Jesus has appointed us to be the light of the world, we have become the reflection and expression of Heaven to this world. When we walk in our Father's ways and abide in the Shadow of Life, He envelops us in a haze of brilliancy. It is our closeness to Him that allows our shadows to grow, and as we learn to shadow Him, He will overshadow us—and maybe even make our shadows legendary, too.

THE BULLET POINT

Psalm 91 redefines what it means to walk in another man's shadow. That man and that shadow is the Son of God. As we make our home in Him and meditate on Him under our fig tree, He promises to make His home in us.

ENDNOTES

1. R.K. Harrison, *Introduction to the Old Testament* (Grand Rapids, MI: Eerdmans Publishing Co., 1969), 966.

2. See Isaiah 36:16; Micah 4:4; and Zechariah 3:10.

3. Merrill C. Tenney, *John: The Gospel of Belief* (Grand Rapids, MI: Eerdmans Publishing Co., 1948), 81-82.

4. See Isaiah 49:2; 51:16.

5. Francis Frangipane, *The Shelter of the Most High* (Lake Mary, FL: Charisma House, 2008), 11.

6. Andrew Murray, *The Believer's Secret of Obedience* (Minneapolis, MN: Bethany House Publishers, 1982), 19.

7. See James 2:23.

8. James Strong, *Biblesoft's New Exhaustive Strong's Numbers and Concordance with Expanded Greek-Hebrew Dictionary* (Nashville, TN: Thomas Nelson Inc., 1994), #G1982.

9. See Genesis 1:2.

10. See Luke 1:35.

11. See Matthew 17:1-9.

CHAPTER 4

DELIVERANCE

*"Surely He shall **deliver you** from the snare of the fowler and from the perilous pestilence"* (Psalm 91:3).

WHEN THE city of Jerusalem was overthrown by the Roman Empire in AD 70, little was left alive. General Titus was merciless. During the six-month siege and subsequent invasion, nearly 1.1 million Jews perished. Those who survived were either carried off as war slaves or imprisoned to be sacrificed in the games of the Coliseum.[1] The fall of Jerusalem in the first century was yet another dark and devastating chapter in the history of the Jewish people, prolonging the Diaspora by another 1,900 years.

During the siege, the conditions inside the walls of the city grew terribly grim. Josephus, a Jewish historian, describes how desperate the situation had become. He writes:

"Throughout the city people were dying of hunger in large numbers, and enduring unspeakable sufferings. In every house the merest hint of food sparked violence, and close relatives fell to blows, snatching from one another the pitiful supports of life. No respect was paid even to the dying. Gaping with hunger, like mad dogs, lawless gangs went staggering and reeling through the streets, battering upon the doors like drunkards, and so bewildered that they broke into the same house two or three times in an hour. Need drove the starving to gnaw at anything. Refuse which even animals would reject was collected and turned into food. In the end they were eating belts and shoes and the leather stripped off their shields. Tufts of withered grass were devoured, and sold in little bundles for four drachmas."[2]

Josephus then recounts a harrowing story about a woman who killed, cooked and consumed her own child. While the account is grisly, I retell it here only to illustrate the profound accuracy of prophetic Scripture. Josephus continues:

"Among the residents of the region beyond Jordan was a woman called Mary, daughter of Eleazar, of the village of Bethezuba (the name means 'House of Hyssop'). She was well off, and of good family, and had fled to Jerusalem with her relatives, where she became involved with the siege. Most of the property she had brought with her had been plundered by the tyrants, and the rest of her treasure, together with such foods as she had been able to procure, was being carried by their henchmen in their daily raids. In her bitter resentment the poor woman cursed and abused these extortioners, and this incensed them against her. However, no one put her to death either from exasperation or pity.

"She grew weary of trying to find food for her kinsfolk. In any case, it was by now impossible to get any, wherever you tried. Famine gnawed at her vitals, and the fire of rage was ever fiercer than famine. So, driven by fury and want, she committed a crime against nature. Seizing her child, an infant at the breast, she cried, 'My poor baby, why should I keep you alive in this world of war and famine? Even if we live till the Romans come, they will make slaves of us; and anyway, hunger will get us before slavery does; and the rebels are crueler than both. Come, be food for me, and an avenging fury to the rebels, and a tale of cold horror to the world to complete the monstrous agony of the Jews.' With these words she killed her son, roasted the body, swallowed half of it, and stored the rest in a safe place.

"But the rebels were on her at once, smelling roasted meat, and threatening to kill her instantly if she did not produce it. She assured them she had saved them a share, and revealed the remains of her child. Seized with horror and stu-pefaction, they stood paralyzed at the sight. But she said, 'This is my own child, and my own handiwork. Eat, for I have eaten already. Do not show yourselves weaker than a woman, or more pitiful than a mother. But if you have pious scru-ples, and shrink away from human sacrifice, then what I have eaten can count as your share, and I will eat what is left as well.' At that they slunk away, trembling, not daring to eat, although they were reluctant to yield even this food to the mother. The whole city soon rang with the abomination. When people heard of it, they shuddered, as though they had done it themselves."[3]

VESPASIAN THE MULETEER

Although Titus is credited with conquering Jerusalem, it was Titus' father Vespasian who initiated the military campaign against the City of David. At that time, Vespasian was a successful military leader in the Roman Empire, and in spring AD 67 Emperor Nero sent Vespasian to quell the mounting Judean revolt. Vespasian assembled an army of 600,000 and in just a few months had quickly and decisively subdued Palestine, Galilee and the cities surrounding Jerusalem. He then made plans for the strategic encirclement of Zion.[4] He even rode his cavalry up to the walls of the city in June AD 68 but then mysteriously rode away.[5] That mystery would soon be revealed.

It was obvious to those around him that Vespasian was distracted by the events happening in Rome. The empire was in turmoil. After an unsuccessful and costly war, several revolts had broken out in the occupied regions. Inter-nally, a conspiracy led by Gaius Calpurnius Piso was launched against Nero but thwarted. Seneca and his nephew Lucan, the epic poet, were among the forty-one prominent Romans implicated in the plot and executed.

Nero Caesar, the fifth emperor of Rome, was notorious for his brutal, cal-lous, and cold-hearted slaughtering of his own people. It is said that he once exe-cuted a man only to steal his wife and was known to have kicked several people to death, including his first wife. It was widely rumored that he even had his own mother clubbed and stabbed to death.[6]

Nero had a special hatred for Jews and Christians, of whom Paul was martyred. Blaming them for the Great Fire of Rome, he had some Christians sewn into skins of wild beasts and thrown to ravenous dogs. Others he dressed in shirts soaked with wax, set them on fire, and used the glow of their burning corpses as torches at night for his garden.[7] Needless to say, Nero was not well loved even by the Romans.

In A.D 68 Gallic and Spanish legions, along with the Praetorian Guards, rose up against the evil emperor, and the senate declared Nero an enemy of the State. He fled Rome but committed suicide on June 9, AD 68.[8] Nero's death would prove to be timely.

At the time of Nero's death, Vespasian was still occupied with plans against Jerusalem, but when Aulus Vitellius assumed power in spring AD 69, Vespasian revolted against Vitellius' claim to the throne. Vespasian marched his armies back to Rome and soon became the new emperor. According to Tacitus, a Roman senator, Vespasian was granted all the honors and privileges of emperor on December 22, AD 69.[9]

In his absence, Vespasian left his son Titus in charge of the occupation of Judea. Several months after his succession to the throne, Emperor Vespasian gave orders for his son to sack the Holy City. Titus began the siege on Passover in April AD 70, and on the 143rd day of the siege, the ninth of Av, the city was taken. Three hundred thousand troops ravaged the city, leveling everyone and everything, including the holy Temple.[10]

EXODUS OF A REMNANT

To the followers of Yeshua Messiah living in Jerusalem, the destruction of the city did not come as a surprise. Christ clearly warned of its destruction, prophesying:

> *"But when you see Jerusalem surrounded by armies, then know that its desolation is near. Then let those who are in Judea flee to the mountains, let those who are in the midst of her depart, and let*

not those who are in the country enter her. For these are the days of vengeance, that all things which are written may be fulfilled. But woe to those who are pregnant and to those who are nursing babies in those days! For there will be great distress in the land and wrath upon this people. And they will fall by the edge of the sword, and be led away captive into all nations. And Jerusalem will be trampled by Gentiles until the times of the Gentiles are fulfilled" (Luke 21:20-24).

About the Temple, Jesus added, "The time is coming when all these things will be completely demolished. Not one stone will be left on top of another" (Luke 21:6 NLT).

The destruction of Jerusalem happened just as Jesus had foretold, and history reveals that the early believers did indeed heed their Master's words. According to Eusebius, a bishop and church historian of the fourth century, followers of the Way fled Jerusalem before the war began and settled in one of the cities of Decapolis east of Galilee. He writes, "The people of the church of Jerusalem had been commanded by a revelation, given to approved men before the war, to leave the city and to dwell in a certain town of Perea called Pella."[11] Some believers, however, still remained in Jerusalem after Vespasian had surrounded the city.

As the occupation progressed, leaving Jerusalem became considerably more difficult for those who remained. Jewish revolutionaries patrolled the outskirts of the city and were not kind to deserters. They were known to slit the throats of those attempting to flee the city. Once the siege began, not only would a person have to survive both famine and food poisoned by the Romans, they also would have to elude the Roman soldiers encamped outside the walls in any attempted escape. It was not uncommon for the soldiers to cut open the stomachs of deserting Jews looking for swallowed gold.

Not only did Jesus forewarn the early church about the fate of Jerusalem, but He gave a prophetic precursor for their deliverance as well. He said, "When you see Jerusalem surrounded by armies...flee to the mountains" (Luke 21:20-21).

When Vespasian marched back to Rome to secure his crown, a window of opportunity unexpectedly opened for the remaining followers of Yeshua. Nero's death had created a way for the early believers to escape the city. History reveals that during this lull, another wave of believers fled the city in summer AD 69. Josephus writes, "Moreover, at the feast which we call Pentecost as the priests were going by night into the inner court of the temple…they felt a quaking and heard a sound as of a multitude saying, 'Let us remove hence.'"[12] Eusebius adds, "For when the city was about to be captured and sacked by Rome, all the disciples were warned beforehand by an angel to remove from the city, doomed as it was to utter destruction. On migrating from it, they settled in Perea."[13]

The Lord used several signs to confirm that Jerusalem was about to be destroyed—a prophecy, an earthquake and an angel. Because the church paid close attention to the words of Christ and the signs from Heaven, God protected them from danger and spared them from His judgment. Unfortunately, those who were not listening to the voice of the Lord did not fare as well.

JERUSALEM'S CASTIGATION

Jerusalem was on a collision course with destruction, but why? Couldn't the city have been spared for the sake of the elect?

Scripture does give some indication. Deuteronomy 28 outlines the blessings of obedience to God's Word and the curses of disobedience. One of the curses listed in this chapter is strikingly similar to the story of the woman who cannibalized her son. It reads:

> *"They shall besiege you at all your gates until your high and fortified walls, in which you trust, come down throughout all your land….You shall eat the fruit of your own body, the flesh of your sons and your daughters whom the LORD your God has given you, in the siege and desperate straits in which your enemy shall distress you. The sensitive and very refined man among you will be hostile toward his brother, toward the wife of his bosom,*

and toward the rest of his children whom he leaves behind, so that he will not give any of them the flesh of his children whom he will eat, because he has nothing left in the siege and desperate straits in which your enemy shall distress you at all your gates. The tender and delicate woman among you…will refuse to the husband of her bosom, and to her son and her daughter, her placenta which comes out from between her feet and her children whom she bears; for she will eat them secretly for lack of everything in the siege and desperate straits in which your enemy shall distress you at all your gates" (Deuteronomy 28:52-57).

Because the church paid close attention to the words of Christ and the signs from Heaven, God protected them from danger and spared them from His judgment.

God's people had neglected His commandments and disobeyed His voice. The destruction of Jerusalem was a prophesied consequence for their rebellion. Tragic as it was, the God of Peace had forewarned and foresaw these events unfolding on account of their disobedience to His laws.

A second rationale for Jerusalem's demise is found in one of the Gospels. Forty years before its destruction, the leaders of Israel had decidedly rejected Yeshua as the Messiah. Luke records that during the final days of His life, the Son of Man approached Jerusalem, wept over it and said, "If you had known, even you, especially in this your day, the things that make for your peace! But now they are hidden from your eyes. For days will come upon you when your enemies will build an embankment around you, surround you and close you in on every side, and level you, and your children within you, to the ground; and they will not leave in you one stone upon another, because you did not know the time of your visitation" (Luke 19:42-44).

Jerusalem had missed the day of its visitation. What they were waiting for and what they were praying for had arrived, only to be rejected and executed.

The King of Israel was not received in the City of the Great King by those He was appointed to rule. Yeshua was their secret place and the very answer to their prayers, but they despised God's means of salvation. "You denied the Holy One and the Just…and killed the Prince of Life" (Acts 3:14-15a). Much like the prophets before Him, they rejected the heavenly agent designed for their peace and refused to repent, leaving them vulnerable to judgment.

PREVENTATIVE CURE

In addition to protection from danger, Psalm 91 promises the dweller deliverance from danger.

> *"Surely He shall deliver you from the snare of the fowler and from the perilous pestilence"* (Psalm 91:3).

The Most High not only shelters from the storm, but He also rescues. He is both a Defender and a Deliverer. When we find ourselves in a war, He is the Commander of the Armies of the Lord. He blocks sickness and heals it; He frustrates an attack and thwarts it; He precludes the plans of the enemy and foils them. He is both our prevention and our cure.

> *"When you pass through the waters, I will be with you; and through the rivers, they shall not overflow you. When you walk through the fire, you shall not be burned, nor shall the flame scorch you"* (Isaiah 43:2).

> *"…The righteous will come through trouble. … No grave trouble will overtake the righteous…"* (Proverbs 12:13, 21).

The snare of the fowler is likened to the trap of a hunter. It is a hidden trick or trap, a scheme and tactic of the enemy aimed to trip us up and prevent us from trusting in our Fortress. Note that Satan's vision is grand—nothing short of pestilence, plague, and full-scale genocide. He is a destroyer. Some translators translate *deber* (pestilence) as *daabar* (a spoken word). In this reading, deliverance is from evil and slanderous words of the demonic nature. The Septuagint uses "word" or "spell," and Rashi likens "plague" and "scourge" to specific names of demons.[14]

The journey toward eternal life is not without its fair share of trials and afflictions. Just as the Prince of Peace had to suffer many things, so must we. But there is a difference between necessary suffering and unnecessary suffering, and it's the latter that Psalm 91 was written to shield us from.

> *"Therefore whoever hears these sayings of Mine, and does them, I will liken him to a wise man who built his house on the rock: and the rain descended, the floods came, and the winds blew and beat on that house; and it did not fall, for it was founded on the rock. But everyone who hears these sayings of Mine, and does not do them, will be like a foolish man who built his house on the sand: and the rain descended, the floods came, and the winds blew and beat on that house; and it fell. And great was its fall"* (Matthew 7:24-27).

Both the foolish man and the wise man heard the words of Christ. Both their houses were hit hard by the storm, but what separated them was that one was a man of action and the other a man of good information.

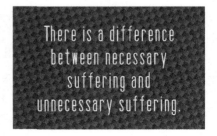

There is a difference between necessary suffering and unnecessary suffering.

Here are some of the ways God chooses to weather us through the storms of life.

1. He removes us from the storm.

The church of Jerusalem found protection from the city's demise by removing itself from the coming day of reckoning. Some scholars believe that out of the over one million Jewish casualties, not one of them was Messianic, meaning a follower of Christ.[15] If true, this is staggering but not completely unprecedented.

Lot was delivered out of Sodom before its destruction. Peter was escorted out of prison by an angel on the eve of his execution. An angel of the Lord appeared to Joseph in a dream, saying, "Arise, take the young Child and His mother, flee to Egypt, and stay there until I bring you word; for Herod will seek the young Child to destroy Him" (Matt. 2:13b).

2. He protects us in the midst of the storm.

Sometimes God's deliverance is His presence. Although we may not be removed altogether from the danger zone, He gives us His abiding peace as an assurance of our safety. It is as if He keeps us hidden in the eye of the storm until the hurricane passes.

Noah walked with God and rode out earth's most epic storm for a year. An angel shut the mouth of the lions when Daniel was thrown in the den. Hananiah, Mishael and Azariah found a fourth man in the fire. Paul and all his shipmates went through the heart of the tempest and were spared.

When the Israelites stood on the banks of the sea after the exodus, not all were convinced that the Deliverer would deliver them. Trapped between a body of water and Pharaoh's pursuing army, they murmured, complained and trembled in fear. Moses assured them, "Do not be afraid. Stand still, and see the salvation of the LORD, which He will accomplish for you today. For the Egyptians whom you see today, you shall see again no more forever. The LORD will fight for you, and you shall hold your peace" (Exod. 14:13-14). We know how that story ended.

Sometimes God takes the occasion of our deliverance as an opportunity to display His greatness. Israel's deliverance from Pharaoh's army was a foregone conclusion in the eyes of Yehovah. Though their crisis was the prevailing issue for the Israelites, it was not the only issue to God. He had in mind their deliverance, but He also had in mind bringing forth a testimony from Pharaoh's downfall. He used their dilemma not only to display His awesome power but also to gain glory for His name: "I will gain honor over Pharaoh and over all his army, that the Egyptians may know that I am [Yehovah]" (Exod. 14:4). This glory is still being celebrated three millenniums later.

Moses could stand confident in the face of fear because this was not the first life-threatening storm he had ever faced. He was given a name that means *drawn out* because he survived a white-water rafting trip in a basket on the Nile as an infant. I guess you could say Moses started out as a basket case! He later would *draw* Israel *out* of Egypt and lead them through the sea on dry ground.

3. He gives us ears to hear the approaching storm.

Yahweh forewarned the believers of the imminent destruction of Jerusalem through an angel, an earthquake, and a prophecy. Because they paid close attention, they were "counted worthy to escape all these things that will come to pass, and to stand before the Son of Man" (Luke 21:36). May this encourage us to know that Heaven communicates in various ways to those with an ear to hear.

We find in Scripture that warning dreams are one way the Spirit of God speaks to us. Pharaoh dreamt of seven years of plenty and seven years of famine. Without it and without the wisdom of Joseph many lives would have been lost, including those of the patriarchs. The magi from the east were warned not to return to Herod through a dream, so they fled using an alternative route. Joseph and Mary settled in Galilee because of a dream warning them from returning to Judea.

When the two angels told Lot to remove himself from the city, he in turn urged his sons-in-law to "get up, get out of this place; for the LORD will destroy this city!" (Gen. 19:14b). Unfortunately they thought he was joking and stayed in the city. Your means of deliverance may come in a package that is unusual or uncomfortable for you, but it is vital that you don't reject His provision because it offends you. It's His prerogative to choose how He secures our protection, and it's our job is to remain close enough to be able to discern it.

4. He rebukes the storm.

> *"Now when He got into a boat, His disciples followed Him. And suddenly a great tempest arose on the sea, so that the boat was covered with the waves. But He was asleep. Then His disciples came to Him and awoke Him, saying, 'Lord, save us! We are perishing!' But He said to them, 'Why are you fearful, O you of little faith?' Then He arose and rebuked the winds and the sea, and there was a great calm. So the men marveled, saying, 'Who can this be, that even the winds and the sea obey Him?'"* (Matthew 8:23-27)

I wonder if Jesus knew the storm was going to hit before He fell asleep. Most likely He did and could have prevented the squall from materializing. Still He falls asleep, knowing full well that His afternoon nap would be interrupted and shortened by His frantic disciples.

We often wonder why God allows us to go through tribulation. It is true. He could have prevented your transmission from going out. He could have secured that job for you. He could have stopped that lawsuit from being filed, but instead He chose to ride out the storm with you. It is usually not until after He delivers us out of the crisis that we realize He had our backs all along. Had there been no test, we may have never marveled at His power and boasted of His goodness, saying, "Who is this marvelous job recruiter, who provides money to replace transmissions and throws lawsuits out of court?"

There is no testimony without a test. Like David running to face Goliath, sometimes our deliverance is found in sprinting toward the giant that approaches. It's the testimony afterward that makes the test worthwhile. The place of your greatest test will become the place of your greatest testimony.

> *"Many are the afflictions of the righteous, but the LORD delivers him out of them all"* (Psalm 34:19).

Psalm 91 is not an insurance policy against the storms of life. It promises instead that we will eventually be delivered from all of them as we place our trust in the Almighty. This means that our troubles are never so desperate that He cannot master them, never so complicated that He can't solve them, and never so tangled that He can't unravel them.

THE BULLET POINT

At the cross some of us were dramatically delivered out of a horrendous and destructive lifestyle. Others were spared from ever having to taste of that destruction. All of us now, though, are saved into an adventurous and spectacular lifestyle. Whether our lives have been sheltered or shattered, it really makes no difference. We all need deliverance from time to time, and Psalm 91 outlines how to secure it: [1] Take refuge under His wings (v. 4); [2] Hold on to truth (v. 4); [3] Do not fear (v. 5); [4] See the reward of the wicked (v. 8); and [5] Know your position over the enemy (v. 13).

How reassuring to know that our well-being is not dependent on medical science, security systems, insurance premiums or flu shots. If we only knew the danger the Lord deflected away from us without our knowledge—the close car wrecks, the near holdups, the seeds of disease circulating in our body—we would surely fall to our knees in utter dependence and thanksgiving. Deliverance is the assurance that gives confidence to the end-time warrior.

ENDNOTES

1. Chuck Missler, "The Book of Revelation," audio teaching series, CD 4.

2. William Whiston, trans., *The Life and Works of Flavious Josephus* (Philadelphia, PA: The John C. Winston Company, 1957), 818-819. This translated English version can be found at http://www.rjgeib.com/thoughts/desolation/josephus.html.

3. Ibid.

4. Flavious Jospehus, *Subjugation of Galilee*, 3.65-4.106; Flavious Josephus, *Siege of Jerusalem*, 4.366-376, 414.

5. "First Jewish-Roman War: Siege of Jerusalem," originally published by MHQ magazine, published online June 12, 2006, http://www.historynet.com/first-jewish-roman-war-siege-of-jerusalem.htm.

6. Nero Claudius Drusus Germanicus (AD 15–AD 68), accessed August 6, 2012, http://www.roman-empire.net/emperors/nero-index.html.

7. Publius Cornelius Tacitus, *The Annals*, 15.33.

8. Encarta Encyclopedia 2000, Microsoft Corporation, 1993–1999.

9. Publius Cornelius Tacitus, *Histories*, 2.76.

10. Flavious Josephus, *Wars of the Jews*, Book 4,9:2; Book 5,5:1ff; http://www.focusonjerusalem.com/thefallofjerusalem.html.

11. Eusebius, *History of the Church*, 3:5:3 (c.325 CE).

12. Josephus, *Wars of the Jews*, 6:5:3.

13. Eusebius, *On Weights and Measures*, 15, (C.4th Century CE).

14. *Oxford Bible Commentary*, (New York, NY: Oxford University Press, 2001), 391.

15. Missler, "The Book of Revelation," CD 4.

CHAPTER 5

WINGS

*"He shall cover you with His feathers, and under His **wings** you shall take refuge; His **truth** shall be your shield and buckler"* (Psalm 91:4).

NOT ONLY does the Almighty have a shadow, but He also has wings. Wings are used figuratively in Scripture to represent protection and transportation.[1]

In this verse, the Most High is likened both to a mother bird protecting its young and to a metal suit of armor. One conveys the intimate touch of a nurturer while the other illustrates the tank-like toughness of a warrior. The secret place of the Most High is both a nest and a bunker. Our Father lovingly cares for us like a hen watching over its chicks and aggressively guards us like an army defending its land. From the perspective of the protected the Lord is gentle, warm, and dove-like in tenderness. From the perspective of the provoker He is intimidating, stronger than steel, and tough as nails.

The imagery of divinely protecting wings is not foreign to Scripture. "I bore you on eagles' wings and brought you to Myself" (Exod. 19:4b). "In the shadow of Your wings I will make my refuge" (Ps. 57:1b). "The woman was given two wings of a great eagle, that she might fly into the wilderness…" (Rev. 12:14).

Each time wings are mentioned a movement is involved—in this case a movement away from peril and a movement toward safety. The metaphor here is of an eagle covering its eaglet and carrying it off to safety on a high rock.[2] The wings of God are designed to transport us from the entanglements of this world and transplant us into the enchantment of His.

WHAT ARE GOD'S WINGS?

In ancient times, Hebrew men wore a rectangular piece of clothing called a tallit, which means *little tent* or *cover*. Usually made of wool, cotton or silk, this four-cornered fringed garment doubled as a prayer shawl. Because six million worshippers couldn't all fit in the Tent of Meeting at the same time, each would use their tallit as a personal sanctuary to meet with the Presence. When pulled up over the head it forms a little cavity, thus the meaning *little tent* or *little tabernacle*. This might be the prayer closet that Jesus is referring to in Matthew 6. Still today Jewish men can be observed wearing a tallit and using it as a prayer tent.

When we read about Elijah's mantle, Scripture is referring to his tallit. When David tore the corner of Saul's robe, he was cutting off the edge of his tallit. Joseph's coat of many colors was likely a bright-striped tallit.

Paul was a tent-maker. We like to presume he was building the first century version of Coleman pup tents in his spare time to make ends meet, but this is not likely. He would have needed a large caravan of camels to carry all the necessary materials to make habitable tents. He was most likely making tallits, a common garment worn in ancient Hebrew culture.

> Jesus is our Kinsman Redeemer who brings His bride under the care and protection of His covering.

At each corner of the tallit knotted tassels called tzitzit are added to the garment. This is done to keep the commandment to "make tassels on the four corners of the clothing with which you cover yourself" (Deut. 22:12). These corners are also referred to as the hem, borders, fringes or wings.[3] When the woman with the issue of blood reached out for the hem of Jesus' garment, she was pulling on His tzitzit or wing.[4] She was expressing her faith in Jesus as the "Sun of Righteousness" who would "arise with healing in His wings" (Mal. 4:2). Perhaps this is the reason her healing stood out to Jesus.

When Ruth uncovered Boaz's feet at the threshing floor, she was requesting her biblical right to marriage and children through a kinsman redeemer. Boaz asked, "Who are you?" and she replied, "I am Ruth, your maidservant. Take your maidservant under your wing, for you are a close relative" (Ruth 3:9). The wing she speaks of is the figurative cover of his tallit. She desired Boaz to spread his authority and protection over her as a husband in accordance with the commandment of Torah.

This custom of spreading the wings of the tallit as a legal covering is still practiced today in orthodox Jewish weddings. The ceremony is typically performed under a *huppah* or *chupa*, which is a large prayer shawl held up by four poles. During the ceremony the groom covers the bride with his tassel-cornered tallit, signifying that he is taking her under his care. Usually this tallit is given to the groom as a wedding gift from his father or father-in-law. So important is this ritual that to cut off the corner of the tallit is regarded as an act of divorce.

The corners of the tallit are called wings, and they represent the Word of God. God's Word is our covering, and Jesus is God's Living Word. He is the One whom we meet with in our little tabernacles and that we reach out to for healing. He wears the coat of many colors and takes up the mantle of Elijah that was given to Him by His heavenly Father. He is our Kinsman Redeemer who brings His bride under the care and protection of His covering.

Scripture is one long revelation of Christ, and the pages of the Bible are the wings that carry us toward Him. We are invited to abide and take refuge in scriptural truth, and as we do we take deeper refuge in Christ. Perhaps this is what the author is conveying when he writes, "Under His wings you shall take refuge; His truth shall be your shield and buckler" (Ps. 91:4b).

THE SWORD AT YOUR SIDE

I have a friend who lives in Kenya. I asked him one day what it was like growing up in Africa. He said, "Oh, Kenya! For one, we are known far and wide for our giant snakes. We have pythons the size of school buses. Some have been known to get up to thirty feet long."

I interrupted, "A thirty-foot-long python? That's not a snake. That's a telephone pole with an attitude!"

He continued, "When I was a boy they would teach us that if a python happens to wrap itself around your leg, quickly find a nearby stick and snap it in half. The snake will think that it has accidentally broken your bone and will loosen its grip. This is your best chance to get out of its hold."

I replied, "Growing up in Africa would be a cultural experience for me. When I was a boy, they taught us to stop, drop and roll."

He then told me about a famous story where he lived. There was a boy shepherd out in the field one day watching over his flock. He sat down in the shade and fell asleep while resting his head against the trunk of the tree. Less than an hour later he awoke staring eye to eye with a gigantic python that had swallowed him up to his mid-section. His legs and feet were immovable and had been sucked whole inside the body of the snake. He would have been swallowed alive had it not been for his sword and sheath that were attached to his belt. As the serpent was ingesting him, the snake couldn't advance past the long scabbard that was sticking out from his body. This smart shepherd proceeded to unsheathe his sword and cut his way out.

Like this story, the Word of God is the tree that we rest under for shelter. When the pythons of life wrap themselves around us, breaking open the Scriptures is a tried and true method of breaking free from their assignment. This is what Jesus did in the desert when tempted by the devil. And if ever we find ourselves half-ingested, immobile and staring eye to eye with Satan himself, we have a sword at our side. Pull it out and use it, for you know what to do with it.

INVESTING IN TRUTH

I've found myself carrying my sword (my Bible) with me more than ever before—not only physically but in my heart. The power of God's Word is no joke. Those, like me, who teach the Scriptures have at times foolishly reduced it to mere good suggestions and positive principles, treating it as if it were some magazine that we flip through or a tidy self-help, coffee-table book. This is a dangerous posture to take.

One of Jesus' favorite phrases was "I tell you the truth." He used it almost eighty times in the Gospels. Paul warns that in the last days some will fall prey to deception through false signs and wonders because they had no love for the truth.[5] A love for the supernatural without a love for truth is a deadly concoction and a recipe for deception. Our spiritual hunger must be coupled with an accompanying passion for truth.

"Buy the truth, and do not sell it" (Proverbs 23:23a).

Making an investment in truth is a wise financial decision. God's Word becomes unbelievably effective when we buy into it and take ownership of it. When we don't, Satan is more than willing to offer us a discounted, wholesale version of truth on the cheap.

I am taking God's Word more seriously than ever before. As a preacher, I am continually reminded that my words may fall to the ground, but only God's Word can truly change a heart. In our marriage, Meljoné and I have agreed to make the Word our arbiter and the final say on any matter. The Bible has proved a worthy marriage counselor, and when my opinion disagrees with the counsel of Scripture, my opinion needs to change. Charles Spurgeon said, "A person whose Bible is falling apart usually has a life that isn't."[6] The same could be said of a marriage.

HEBREW APPROACH

The Hebrew approach to Scripture differs quite a bit from our western Greek approach. We tend to examine the Bible the way any good student would, extracting useful information from it to further our spiritual education. Running it through the scientific method and what we know to be true of life and culture, we seek to wrap our minds around it so we can teach others what we've learned.

This is not how those who have passed down the Scriptures to us study it. To the Hebrews, God's Word is not a textbook for higher education but a manual on how to flesh out their faith. They seek the doing of it more than comprehension of it. Because of this, more emphasis is placed on verbs than nouns, wisdom than knowledge, action than understanding. It's less about head knowledge and more about heart obedience, less the tree of knowledge and more the tree of life. Simply put, they read Scripture to better please God.

We would do well to follow this same approach. The goal of Scripture is not to increase our knowledge but to guide our conduct, "that the man of God may be complete, thoroughly equipped for every good work" (2 Tim. 3:17). We should all make it our goal to read Scripture for the purpose of pleasing God. When and if understanding does come, it is a secondary and blessed by-product.

We will never comprehend all there is to know about the Great I Am and His Word. That's a fact. And if we wait to start putting the Word into practice until we know the why and wherefore of it, we will never reap the benefits it holds for us. Blind obedience credits our Maker with knowing things that we don't and perhaps will never comprehend. By embracing His ways, our understanding of God is given room to grow.

Mark Twain wrote, "Most people are bothered by those passages in Scripture which they cannot understand, but as for me, I always noticed that the passages in Scripture which trouble me the most are those which I do understand."[7]

BY THE BOOK

The famous eighteenth-century French philosopher Voltaire was no lover of Scripture. He was known to gather up all the Bibles he could find and burn them. He predicted that the Holy Bible would eventually pass away from common use. He boasted that within fifty years his book, *Candide*, would sell at a premium while one would not be able to even give away a Bible. As history would tell, exactly fifty years after Voltaire's death the very house he lived in was being used by the Geneva Bible Society to print Bibles. Today it has four presses, publishing thousands of Bibles every year in several dozen languages.[8]

> *"The entirety of Your word is truth, and every one of Your righteous judgments endures forever"* (Psalm 119:160).

> *"Heaven and earth will pass away, but My words will by no means pass away"* (Luke 21:33).

Throughout history many have tried to burn the Bible, but fire has a way of surviving fire. Even though it doesn't make the *New York Times*' best-seller list, the Bible is still always a best-seller year after year. Who could find a book like it? Sixty-six separate books with forty different authors, written over a period of 1,500 years in three different languages, spanning three continents, yet containing no contradictions and has one theme—the redemption of mankind.

Many have burned Bibles, but fire has a way of surviving fire.

Archaeology and the fossil record have verified and confirmed the facts and historical accuracy of the Bible to the minutest degree. This can't be said for other religious books. The discovery of the Dead Sea Scrolls surprised scholars, displaying unbelievable reliability of the Masoretic Text, the manuscript widely used to translate our modern Bible. Additionally, the New Testament has proved to be the most reliable historical document of all time due to the age and sheer number of its earliest manuscripts. The second most reliable documents, the writings of Homer, are not even close. As for prophecy, from Alexander the Great to King Cyrus to the life of Jesus, the number of prophecies fulfilled with pinpoint precision is staggering. No other book has accurately predicted world events and the rise and fall of nations like the Bible has.

One unknown author writes, "The Scriptures are accurate in their descriptions, unfailing in their prophecies, dependable in their promises, reliable in their histories, authoritative in their claims, united in their testimonies, self-evidencing in their miracles, honest in their records, suggestive in their silence, final in their teachings, divine in their origin, unique in their structure, living in their nature, heavenly in their morality, perennial in their freshness and inexhaustible in their depth."[9]

Will Houghton said, "Lay hold of the Bible and the Bible lays hold of you."[10] Here are some ways you and I can lay hold of God's Word and come under its wings.

1. Read it for leisure.

When I was a freshman at San Jose State University, I had to drop out of school for a semester after injuring my left knee while playing basketball. After four surgeries and spending close to six months on crutches, the Holy Spirit used those circumstances to turn my life around. Even though I was saved at an early age, I refer to this time in my life as my "adult conversion." It proved to be a significant spiritual marker in my walk with Christ.

During that season, I had an insatiable appetite for God's Word. To pay for tuition, I worked at an upholstery supply shop and would often bring my Bible to work. When the office was slow I found myself reading whole chapters and books in one sitting. Though they were all stories and verses I grew up learning, for the first time I took ownership of them. Instead of knowing just the facts and contents of Scripture, the Holy Spirit was using them to speak to me.

Did you know that it takes a typical person roughly seventy hours to read the entire Bible through at an average reading rate?[11] That's fifty-two hours to read the Old Testament and another eighteen for the New. Stretched out over the course of a year, that's less than twelve minutes a day to read through the entire Bible. You can do this!

Tennyson wrote, "Bible reading is an education in itself."[12] When I read Scripture for leisure, I read it like I would a novel. I pick it up and start reading where I left off. I suggest using a contemporary, easy-to-read version if possible.

You'll be amazed at how the story of redemption grows richer when you get an overall glimpse of it from cover to cover.

2. Study it for context.

I am not the kind of guy who reads no other book but the Bible. Neither do I read only one version of it. I respect those who do, but I recognize that the English text is a translated document. Since most of us do not speak or read Hebrew and ancient Greek, we are at the mercy of translators. For this reason, I find the use of Bible dictionaries, lexicons, concordances, and commentaries to be useful and necessary. These helps investigate the background and context of a passage and widen understanding of it. Often more clarity is needed, and I've found that the way one particular translation renders a verse is usually not sufficient in itself.

Before you begin a study, start by choosing a topic or book of the Bible that you feel drawn toward. Exhaust all the resources possible when looking to understand it, especially those that hold a different point of view than you. Just like nature, Scripture comes alive when put to the microscope.

3. Memorize it for accessibility.

Have you ever had pieces of a Bible verse come to mind but not remember its address? This happens to all of us and usually when we most need it! Memorizing Scripture can solve that dilemma. A Bible stored in the mind is worth more than a thousand stored on the shelf. I've found that the more Scripture verses I put to memory, the more potent my arsenal is when praying or ministering to someone.

4. Meditate on it for depth.

Most of the nuggets in Scripture that I have come across have been while meditating on one particular verse in depth. Like the turning of a composter, the more we turn over a truth in our thoughts, the richer the soils of our mind become and the deeper its roots penetrate our soul. Try writing a verse down on an index card and keeping it in your pocket for the day, or tape it to your bathroom mirror. As you see it at different times of the day, you will begin to see that truth in a different light as well.

5. Use it as a devotional for prayer.

Usually when a person is struggling to find a prayer vocabulary, it's often due to a Word deficiency. For this, consider using your Bible as a prayer guide. Simply open up it and pray what you read. Commune with God over it, ask Him questions, pray it back to Him. Psalms is a great book for this kind of interaction. Try reading five psalms and one proverb a day. Because there are 150 chapters in Psalms and 31 in Proverbs, you will read each book once a month, twelve times a year. Here the goal is not to accomplish your reading assignment and check it off your to-do list. Take some time and make it a dialogue with the Author.

6. Obey it for life.

> *"Blessed is he who reads and those who hear the words of this prophecy, and keep those things which are written in it; for the time is near"* (Revelation 1:3).

Reading, hearing and understanding are all needed and necessary, but the true treasure of Scripture is found in its application. Our study and memorization become fruitless when we don't put it into action. Make it your aim to always read God's Word with a predetermination to obey what you read and a prayer for grace to perform it.

Here's a good exercise. Find Deuteronomy 10:12-13 and read it out loud. Study it, meditate on it, put it to memory and pray it back to God. Now here's where the fun really begins—put it into practice!

THE BULLET POINT

In English we use the phrase "taken under the wing" to convey when someone has taken it upon him or herself to train and mentor another. The mentee becomes an understudy to the mentor. In the same way, let God's Word take you up and take you under its wings. Let it train, guide, and disciple you in the secret place of your conduct. As we meditate and study Scripture, we become a student and understudy of the Living Word of God.

ENDNOTES

1. Kevin J. Conner, *Interpreting the Symbols and the Types* (Portland, OR: Bible Temple Publishing, 1992), 181.

2. See Deuteronomy 32:11-12; Job 39:27-28.

3. See Numbers 15:38; Ezekiel 16:8.

4. See Mark 5:24-34.

5. See 2 Thessalonians 2:9-12.

6. Charles Spurgeon, accessed August 6, 2012, http://www.goodreads.com/quotes/397346-a-bible-that-s-falling-apart-usually-belongs-to-someone-who.

7. Roy B. Zuck, *The Speaker's Quote Book* (Grand Rapids, MI: Kregal Publications, 1997), 35.

8. Ibid, 31.

9. Ibid, 29.

10. Ibid, 34.

11. Ibid, 38.

12. Ibid, 32.

CHAPTER 6

INVINCIBILITY

*"His truth shall be your **shield** and **buckler"***
(Psalm 91:4c).

As a boy I loved superheroes. My favorites were Batman, Plastic Man, Flash, Green Lantern, Greatest American Hero, and the Six-Million-Dollar Man. One of my most prized possessions was a limited edition Incredible Hulk Stretch-Armstrong action figure. It was not uncommon to see me dashing around the house donning a Lone Ranger mask, clad in Spiderman underoos, spinning webs from my wrists, and using a bath towel as a cape. What boy doesn't dream of being a hero?

In my mind, the best and the bravest of the all superheroes was Superman. He was the ultimate crime-fighting, death-defying defender of the planet. I remember one episode where he interrupts a thief in the middle of a bank robbery. Despite being caught red-handed, the beanie-clad, machine-gun wielding robber takes aim at Superman. To the dismay and frustration of the criminal, the spray of bullets spring off Superman's chest like rubber balls bouncing off a windshield. It was futile to resist. Even a bullet couldn't stop Superman. He was bulletproof.

Still today we buy into the superhero market. Why? Because deep within us is a God-given attraction to something otherworldly. In the comic book world Superman is known as the Metropolis Marvel, the Last Son of Krypton, the Man of Tomorrow, and the Man of Steel. In the real world, however, Jesus is the Man of Steel we should idolize and the Man of Tomorrow we should hope in. He is the Savior of the planet, the King of the world, the Desire of All Nations, the Firstborn from the Dead, the Son of Man, and the Son of God. He is our ultimate Hero and will reveal His true identity to those who seek to know Him. As we worship Him we become like Him: heroes in every sense of the word—heroes to our spouses, heroes to our children, and heroes to our community. Your life now is your moment in history to do something heroic.

KRYPTONITE

Every superhero is not without a weakness though. To Superman it's kryptonite. To Spiderman it's Venom. To Green Lantern it's the color yellow. Read Greek mythology and it becomes evident that our heroes struggle in the same ways we do, probably because we have the tendency to fashion them after our own image. This is the problem with our superheroes. They don't always act heroically.

But Jesus was perfect in all His ways because He was fashioned in the image of God. He had no weakness that His enemies could take advantage of. "The ruler of this world is coming, and he has nothing in Me" (John 14:30b). Hebrews declares that Jesus came in "the power of an indestructible life" (Heb. 7:16 NIV). Like Superman, He is unstoppable. Unlike Superman, however, He has no kryptonic weakness. Even death could not put an end to His reign of dominance.

In the Gospels, Jesus displayed superhuman abilities, demonstrating dominion over the forces of nature, the forces of evil, and the power of death. His clothing could heal the sick, not to mention His saliva. He supplied money from the mouth of a fish to pay His taxes and commanded a whole school of tilapia to jump into Peter's net. He brought new meaning to the term "deviled ham" when

He sent raging demons into rural swine. And that's just the beginning. John supposed that the world could not contain the books written about the works of Yeshua of Nazareth, and He is still building upon His résumé.

Jesus was bulletproof in every sense of the word. Once, after hearing Him preach, an angry mob forced Him to a steep cliff at the edge of town. Armed with whips and stones they intended to punish Him thoroughly, if not execute Him for His controversial teachings. This was no court of law. It was a mob scene, and Galileans were notorious for this kind of behavior.

Mind you, these men weren't the riffraff of society. They were the elders of the synagogue, the spiritual leaders of the region, the fathers of the faith. What upset them most was Jesus' audacity to suggest that the God of Abraham, Isaac, and Jacob was extending covenantal rights to the Gentiles. I can envision one saying, "Who does He think He is?" and another tearing his garments, shouting, "Blasphemy." Yet, the Prince of Peace remained vigilant. He knew who He was and where He was going.

Jesus was bulletproof in every sense of the word.

Luke records how the incident ends. In the midst of this violent crowd, Jesus turns around and strolls through—untouched, unfazed, and unharmed. Just like that He escapes danger and goes on about His day. When I picture this story, I envision the multitude suddenly hushing and parting like the Red Sea as they seek to capture Jesus. His accusers stand paralyzed, dumbfounded, and helpless. It would seem like something right out of comic book folklore if it weren't history.[1]

This would not be the last time the Jews would try to kill their Messiah or the only time their plans would be foiled. Jesus had an uncanny ability to escape arrest, avoid being stoned, and elude the attacks of His adversaries. He even once made Himself essentially invisible to flee from His opponents in the Temple.[2]

Jesus was immortal. When an army of soldiers sought to arrest Him in the garden of Gethsemane, one word from His mouth knocked all of them off their feet and pinned them to the ground. It was as if He wanted to demonstrate that

He would not be arrested apart from the sovereign timing of His Father. It was His mercy that the soldiers only tasted a drop of His infinite power instead of being annihilated by it.

BULLETPROOF VEST

As followers of Christ, we should expect no less in the face of danger. The Father of our Lord Jesus Christ is our protector from dangerous men, dangerous times, and dangerous situations. Some may argue that Jesus escaped His captors naturally, not supernaturally. Whether natural or supernatural, it makes no difference. The Defender protected Him until His appointed time with death.

For us, it should make no difference either. Whether our Father protects us from an intruder through an alarm or an angel, it is still His protection. If God's provision for us is a well-paying job or money falling from the sky, it is still His provision. His work does not have to be supernatural to be effective, yet it is not confined to mere natural solutions either. Whether natural or supernatural, our lives become naturally supernatural in Christ, and dwelling in the secret place assures us that our appointment with death will not come prematurely.

> If truth is our spiritual armor, then righteousness is our bulletproof vest.

What made Jesus invincible? Peter reveals that He "'committed no sin, nor was deceit found in His mouth'; who, when He was reviled, did not revile in return; when He suffered, He did not threaten, but committed Himself to Him who judges righteously" (1 Pet. 2:22-23). Satan had no dirt on Jesus; therefore, he had no hold on Him. The devil could not so much as even breathe on the Son of Man because He was full of truth and righteousness.

Truth and righteousness are major themes running throughout Scripture. Psalm 91 is no exception. The psalmist writes, "His truth shall be your shield and buckler" (Ps. 91:4c). Solomon said, "He who speaks truth declares righteousness" (Prov. 12:17a). Paul adds, "Stand therefore, having girded your waist with truth, having put on the breastplate of righteousness" (Eph. 6:14). If truth is our spiritual armor, then righteousness is our bulletproof vest. With them we are twice-armored.

God's truth is a coating that guards our innermost being, and His righteousness is a flak jacket that protects our hearts. They toughen our skin and soften our hearts. When we are wrapped up in His truth and righteousness, we are given the innate ability to recognize and resist the flaming arrows of the enemy. His fiery darts bounce harmlessly off us like rubber balls off Superman's chest.

ELISE

When I was a campus missionary, a girl named Elise became involved in our ministry at Chico State and served as a student leader in our fellowship. Elise was small in stature but strong in faith and had a big heart. While attending a youth and prayer conference in Washington, D.C., some intercessors prayed over her and prophesied that Psalm 91 would carry her through this next season of her life. Little did she know what awaited her when she returned home to Northern California.

Three days after arriving back in Chico, Elise was bringing in groceries from her car. A man walked up to her apartment door, saying, "Excuse me. Do you know if your neighbors are home?" He used their first names and said they were his friends. Elise knew these particular neighbors, and when she told him they were not home he asked if he could use her home telephone to call them. She obliged and went downstairs to park her car. When she came back up, he handed her the phone saying that he couldn't reach them. As she was escorting him to the door, he kicked the door shut, grabbed her by the wrists and began to force her down the hallway.

A struggle ensued. Furniture was damaged, walls were marked, and a mirror fell to the floor. Unable to free herself from his grasp, she kept hoping someone would see the assault through the open blinds and rescue her. Unfortunately nobody did. He forced her to the ground in her bedroom and sat on top of her.

He tried to kiss her multiple times, but she kept moving her head away from his advances.

Elise recounts, "I was in total shock at this point, thinking this must just be an awful dream. But after he had me pinned to the floor, I woke up and realized it was no dream. I needed to fight back, for I was about to lose my virginity through being raped. No matter how hard I tried to resist him, it was futile. He was simply too strong for me."

Elise figured her only other recourse was to talk to him, so she told him all about Jesus. She said that God loved him, had something better for him and that he was not meant to be doing this. She conveyed the gospel to him, but this only made him angry. He grew so livid that he began to strangle her, but just as she started to lose her breath he let go.

He then took a razor blade to her neck, held it there tightly and told her to "Shut up!" Elise writes, "It worked. I shut up. I was too young and had too many dreams to pursue, and I did not want to lose my life this day or in this way."

She recounts, "I was helpless. Lying there with my arms pinned to ground, I came to the end of my rope. My strength could not save me. My words could not save me, and no one was coming to rescue me. Just like my salvation, only Christ could save me now, and I had to rely on the Holy Spirit to free me from this awful predicament. I found myself crying out to Him in my heart, asking for His intervention and surrendering my life once again to His will."

"From that point on," she describes, "everything changed. I looked up at this guy whom I was expected to kick and punch and hate, and as crazy as it sounds I felt compassion for him. I felt the Father's heart for a young man who really didn't know what he was doing, a guy who was lost in a world full of confusion and pain. I saw him as someone's son and as a person designed to know the love of the heavenly Father. In that moment the Holy Spirit moved upon my heart, and I kept asking him simply, 'Can I help you?'"

What happened next was nothing short of miraculous. Her attacker's countenance changed from anger to remorse. He began to feel the presence and urgings of the Holy Spirit. Visibly, he showed grief over what he was doing. It was a shocking turnaround. Just as Elise responded to God's heart of compassion for this guy, in turn he responded to God's heart of compassion for her!

"I asked him to toss the razor blade in the closet, which I opened with my free arm, telling him I wanted to talk to him. At first he resisted but then slid the blade into his back pocket. He started to apologize to me, saying he was sorry and that he didn't mean to do this. I asked him to get off of me so we could talk and finally he relented. Grace filled the room. I felt it. He felt it. I told him that God forgives him. He said 'Yea, repentance.' He knew what was going on and so did I."

"We talked about forgiveness, and he asked me for a hug. I gave him a nice side hug, and he said that it wasn't a good hug. I told him it was my hug for that moment, which he respected. It was as if he knew he couldn't do anything except what the Holy Spirit deemed permissible for that moment. He then told me that he would leave if I would get under the bed, but I refused. I informed him that I was going to stand where I was standing and he could leave."

"After he left, I called my pastor and then the police. The district attorney and all the officers were astounded at my story. Upon some investigation, they identified the young man and arrested him that evening."

"I stayed at my pastor's house that night, and as I closed my eyes all I could see was this young man. Unable to sleep, I opened my Bible, and it fell open to Psalm 91. There it was—my testimony! The Psalmist was describing exactly what had happened to me, just as the intercessors had foretold. No one was able to harm me because I was safe under His wings of protection."

That week Chico State's school newspaper printed her story in the Orion but spun it to infer that Elise saved herself through her quick-witted communication. Elise promptly called the paper and set the record straight, praising the presence of God, and quoting Psalm 91. Amazingly, they corrected the story and reposted it. For several weeks she had girl after girl come up to her with their personal stories of rape and abuse. On each occasion she was able to pray for grace and healing to penetrate their hearts.

A year later, the young man was convicted and served time in state prison. As it turned out, he had raped two other girls prior. At the trial, Elise says, "The

Holy Spirit brought this phrase to mind just as I was about to testify, 'A thousand may fall at your side, ten thousand at your right hand, but it will not come near you. You will only observe with your eyes and see the punishment of the wicked.' I am a living testimony of the power of the secret place, all because the Living Word Himself was in the room that day. The God of Psalm 91 is faithful to be who He says He is. He keeps His Word no matter how difficult the situation someone may find themselves in."

THE BULLET POINT

The book of Acts is full of stories of God's protection of our forefathers. Paul escaped a murderous plot by being let down over the wall of Damascus in a basket.[3] An angel opened the prison doors and instructed the apostles to "stand in the temple and speak to the people all the words of this life."[4] The Jews stoned Paul, dragged him out of the city of Lystra and left him for dead, but he stood up and went back in the city when the disciples gathered around him.[5]

Jesus is bulletproof and so is His bride. He is invincible and so is His blood. Our Hero was a show-stopping, game-changer who walked in the perfect will of God, which made Him untouchable. Just as the Father delivered Him and the early church from danger through natural and supernatural means, so we can fearlessly trust God's protection from wicked men and the reward that awaits them. Righteous truth is a spiritual armor for the end-time warrior.

ENDNOTES

1. See Luke 1:16-30.

2. See John 7:30, 44; 8:59; 10:39; 18:6.

3. See Acts 9:23-25.

4. See Acts 5:20.

5. See Acts 14:19-20.

CHAPTER 7

FEARLESS

*"You shall **not be afraid** of the terror by night, nor of the arrow that flies by day, nor of the pestilence that walks in darkness, nor of the destruction that lays waste at noonday"* (Psalm 91:5-6).

THE INDUSTRY of fear is big business these days. Worldwide box office numbers reached an all-time high at $29.4 billion in 2009 and $31.8 billion in 2010, only to be surpassed at $32.6 billion in 2011.[1] At a time when the film industry is recording record highs each year, a new horror flick is released every 40.7 seconds.[2] Not surprisingly and probably linked, anxiety-related diseases continue to escalate. According to the National Institute of Mental Heath, one in eight Americans between the ages of eighteen and fifty-four have an anxiety disorder. Anxiety is now the most common "disorder" in the U.S., affecting forty million Americans or roughly eighteen percent of the population.[3] Studies show that anxiety treatment and coping methods cost the American people $42 billion a year.[4] What is more, the National Institute of Mental Health reports that one in ten people are plagued by a specific phobia.[5]

Clinical phobias like acrophobia (fear of heights), dentophobia (fear of dentists), trypanophobia (fear of injections), xenophobia (fear of strangers), herpetophobia (fear of creepy, crawly things) and thanatophobia (fear of death or dying) are not uncommon. What is alarming, however, is the rising number of phobias. It seems there are just about as many phobias as folks these days.

Take, for example, some of the more unusual yet documented phobias: Consecotaleophobia (fear of chopsticks), porphyrophobia (fear of the color purple), omphalophobia (fear of belly buttons), pentheraphobia (fear of mother-in-law), anemophobia (fear of air), automatonophobia (fear of a ventriloquist's dummy), phalacrophobia (fear of becoming bald), defecaloesiophobia (fear of painful bowel movements), politicophobia (fear of politicians), barophobia (fear of gravity), pteronophobia (fear of being tickled by feathers), paraskavedekatriaphobia (fear of Friday the thirteenth), gamophobia (fear of marriage), zemmiphobia (fear of The Great Mole Rat) and hexakosioihexekontahexaphobia (fear of 666). If that doesn't cover it, then panophobia (fear of everything) or phobophobia (fear of fear) will.

Fear is insanity, and Psalm 91 offers a calming voice of reason. It not only promises protection from impending danger but also from the fear of impending danger. This is because the fear of evil has the potential to be just as paralyzing as evil itself.

COWARDLY AND UNBELIEVING

Revelation 21:8 describes the kind of people who will inhabit hell. It's not lite-reading material for sure. Included are the corrupt, the murderer, the immoral, the sorcerer, the idolater, and the liar, but at the top of the list are the cowardly and unbelieving. We often don't view fear and unbelief as evil attributes. We might think of them as struggles, foibles or weaknesses, but not hell-sending wickedness. The Bible thinks otherwise.

Unbelief, particularly in God's Son, prevents us from the reward of salvation, and fear is always the first step toward unbelief. Peter began to sink when he began to fear. The unprofitable servant hid his talent out of fear. Fear is not only toxic in what it puts us in bondage to, but also in what it causes us to run to for refuge. It is a sobering thought to know that God will judge us both for what we do and for who we refuse to become due to fear.

When Adam and Eve ate the forbidden fruit, fear was an immediate consequence of their sin. Scripture records that they were afraid and hid from the presence of God. Humans had never experienced fear until this moment, and we have been fighting it ever since.

BIG BRIAN

Growing up, I wasn't much of a fighter. There's a word for this. It's called being a wimp! One of my first fights was with Brian in the third grade. He and I got sent to the principal's office for fighting, if you can call it that. It was more like I got busted for getting busted up!

Big Brian was the biggest and strongest kid in our class. If I didn't know better I would figure he was the only eight-year-old in our school on steroids. One day while standing in line to get into class, he got upset with me and punched me in the face. I then remember him rolling his hands inside his jacket sleeves and using my head as his personal punching bag. Being the good Christian kid that I was, I turned the other cheek, as well as the other chin, nose, lip, ear, and eye socket. It wasn't that I was so spiritual. It was that I was too scared to fight back.

It was the classic story of David versus Goliath, except this time David lost. Eventually, our teacher rescued me and sent us to see the principal. Brian got in trouble for fighting, and I got in trouble for getting pulverized!

Psalm 91 is the antidote to intimidation. It injects us with the courage to stand up to our giants and assures us that neither Goliath nor Big Brian is bigger than the Great and Mighty One. Not only was David the only one with the guts to fight Goliath, but Scripture records that he sprinted to the battlefield to face him. A boy standing before a nine-foot, nine-inch sasquatch. But David knew something

Fear is insanity.

the Philistines didn't. He knew Goliath wasn't bulletproof! Most would think, "He's so big. How can I win?" Not David. He probably thought, "He's so big. How can I miss?" Fear has a way of warping our perspective. Like me in the third grade, the fight is over before it even begins when we are too afraid to come out swinging.

UNDEFEATED FEAR

One of the battles I've had to contend with has been the giant of discouragement. We all have targeted weapons fashioned against us, and for me it has been fear in the form of discouragement. Discouragement doesn't show up on my doorstep and say, *Remember me? Let's get back together.* It's more subtle than that. It typically sneaks its way into my thinking through the avenue of a disappointment, and as I linger on that disappointment, discouragement follows. The more I feed into discouragement, the more I inch closer to depression and despair. I have learned that I can break the cycle of depression by properly dealing with discouragement in its earliest stages.

Depression is the common cold of psychological disorders. The National Institute of Mental Health calls depression the number one health problem in America.[6] In the past few years, there has been a shocking increase of clinical depression among preschoolers, as the latest reports show a sharp twenty-three percent increase among young children every year.[7] According to the World Health Organization (WHO), depression affects 120 million people worldwide.

Depression is a self-inflicted wound. It is anger turned inward. Spiritually speaking, depression is caused by fearful anxiety about our self-esteem, as Proverbs says "Anxiety in the heart of man causes depression" (Prov. 12:25a). Depression is a heart issue and is the demonic progression of discouragement.

In Numbers 21, the children of Israel found themselves woefully discouraged and at one of their lowest points since leaving Egypt. It was the thirty-ninth year of their wilderness wandering. Frustrated and battle-weary, they were off course and forced to take a detour that led them deeper into the desert. Moses, having just buried his sister Miriam, was informed he would not be leading Israel into the Promised Land due to his unbelief. The people were tired, hot, hungry, impatient and sick of "McManna" sandwiches. Scripture says, "The soul of the people became very discouraged..." (Num. 21:4b).

On top of it all they were stuck—stuck between their promise and their past. They had drifted as nomads for almost four decades and were still a year away from entering Canaan. They were no longer slaves in Egypt, yet not quite home free. They were caught between their past and their future, between yesterday and tomorrow. They were not who they used to be yet not whom they were called to be. Living in the here and now, they found themselves homeless, restless, aimless, purposeless, jobless, and unsettled.

Life was difficult for Israel. The terrain they walked was very rugged and the conditions were hot and trying. What is more, the path they were on was in the opposite direction of the Promised Land. The Edomites, descendants of Esau and cousins to the Israelites, had refused to allow them passage through their land. At their breaking point, they vented their frustrations on Moses and lashed out against God, who sent poisonous snakes to strike them.

Like Israel, life may be difficult for you. Perhaps you find yourself in transition, wandering in the desert and stuck in your circumstances—stuck between where you've been and where you're going. The path you walk today may seem extremely rugged and trying. Broken relationships and dysfunction have led you away from your dreams and further into the wilderness, forcing you on a detour you never intended to take. Maybe you feel aimless, passionless, without purpose, without a home, and without vision.

God had a plan for bringing Israel out of their discouragement. He led them past the Red Sea on their journey around Edom. Perhaps they needed a reminder of God's past faithfulness, victory, and deliverance, as well as an assurance that His promise is just around the corner. He does the same with us. He reminds us of our past, and as we remember the trial we also remember the triumph of our Redeemer.

When discouraged, it is important to not forget where you've been and where you're going. Our hope in Him is what pulls us through the hardships of life. If we will allow Him, God can change our past from being a hammock that we slink back into, to a springboard that launches us into our destiny.

When the Israelites came confessing their sins and asking for the snakes to be taken away, Moses made a bronze serpent upon God's instruction and put it on a pole. Everyone who had been bitten and looked upon the image lived. Jesus likened Himself to that bronze image, saying, "And as Moses lifted up the serpent in the wilderness, even so must the Son of Man be lifted up, that whoever believes in Him should not perish but have eternal life" (John 3:14-15). That this statement heralds the most famous Scripture of all time is no mistake. It highlights the fact that Jesus became a curse for us so that we no longer need to live under the curse of fear, sin, depression, disease, and death.

God can change our past from being a hammock to a springboard.

Discouragement and depression are paralyzing because they are rooted in a spirit of fear. To be *dis*-couraged means to be separated from your courage. Discouragement is simply a result of undefeated fear in our lives and usually follows a decision to delay an action.

ALLERGIES: A LEARNED FEAR

Besides discouragement, another side effect to walking in fear is allergies, something I am all too familiar with. Skin allergies, food allergies and hay fever all have their root in the unholy trinity of fear, worry and anxiety.

Here's how allergies work. When someone with allergies is exposed to an allergen, their immune system releases a special type of antibody to counteract it. These antibodies lead other cells to release histamines and together they form an allergic reaction. Allergenic symptoms such as itching, sneezing, wheezing, swelling, congestion, diarrhea, watery eyes, and a runny nose is the body's attempt at flushing out the irritant and delivering itself from the antigen. This is why many allergy medications include an antihistamine component to treat the symptoms.

The problem with allergies is that they are an unnecessary reaction; they are the result of a hypersensitive immune system. In other words, there is no need for our bodies to have such a strong reaction. The immune system is fooled into believing that a normally innocuous substance is a dangerous invader. It mis-identifies something benign as harmful and sends far too many antibodies to the scene, bombarding it with a force much greater than required.

To illustrate, suppose your sister is allergic to dog hair and stops by a friend's apartment to meet her new roommate who owns a dog. The place is crawling with dog hair, and immediately upon her arrival the skin around her nose begins to itch and she starts to sneeze. What is happening is that her immune system is having a hypersensitive reaction to the dander from the dog hair. Her body is overreacting and secreting antibodies to counteract the antigen. Dander is not the cause of her sneezing and itching but rather it is the fearful response of her immune system.

According to Henry Wright in his book *A More Excellent Way,* allergies are an absolute rip-off. Medically speaking, he argues that our bodies should not be allergic to anything and contends that we are created to be compatible with our environment. Dander is not toxic; neither is mold, wheat, milk, peanuts, sugar, cinnamon sugar, or pollen. Our bodies were formed from the dust of the ground, so being allergic to dust is counterintuitive and contradicts the creative order. We should not naturally be allergic to things that our Creator has created for us to enjoy.

Like fear, allergies cause our bodies to overreact to something that is non-threatening. Where does the body learn this? From our souls, of course. When we react in fear to our environment, so will our body. When we become anxious about something new or unfamiliar to us, our immune system follows suit. Our bodies mimic the behavior of our emotions. Since our souls are the captains of our being, our body learns to react in fear from us.

When I allow myself to worry about God's provision or protection for my family, I am giving my immune system permission to worry as well. When I'm anxious about a new job, relationship or potential risk, I am sending signals to my immune system to do likewise when faced with something new. My immune system is picking up on my hypersensitive reaction to my environment and copying it. In this way, allergies are a learned fear.

Have you noticed that allergies have a way of taking over if allowed to go unchecked? What starts out as dry skin develops into hives and eczema. What begins as lactose intolerance evolves into allergies to nuts, wheat and gluten. Soon, a full array of allergies is dictating what a person can or cannot eat and where he or she can or cannot go.

Fear works in the same way. Although we may not be afraid of the bogey man anymore, fear finds other ways to manifest itself through the fear of failure, rejection, abandonment, disease or other people's opinions. Fear attempts to dictate our behavior and will get away with it if left unchecked. You must know that fear will not leave by itself or fade away with age. It matures as we mature because fear is a spirit.

Paul writes, "God has not given us a spirit of fear" (2 Tim. 1:7a). John adds, "...Perfect love casts out fear..." (1 John 4:18a). I have found the best way to deal with fear and allergies is to cast it out as you would any other spirit and replace it with power, love and a sound mind. Sometimes I do this on a daily basis.

Here is a prayer I use when battling allergy symptoms. I've found it to be effective.

> *Heavenly Father, I confess the sin of fear, worry, anxiety and stress. I repent of these and renounce them. I identificationally confess and repent of every inherited or generational link to fear, worry and anxiety, and I completely renounce it. Father, show me where I have taken up fear. I bind fear, generational fear, worry, generational worry, anxiety, generational anxiety, stress, generational stress from me, and cast it off of me, out of me, away from me; you get behind me. Fear, get out of my DNA, RNA and my entire being. You will not shape my personality. You will go to where Yeshua of Nazareth sends you and nowhere else. You will*

not pass on to my children, grandchildren or to their children. I speak to my antibodies and histamines. Stop being released. I declare that my body is not allergic to dust, mold, mildew, pollen, ragweed, grass, or any foods that I am designed to eat. Amen.

WHO TAUGHT US TO BE AFRAID?

Once during another epic match of hide-and-go-seek with my kids, my son and I snuck into the downstairs closet to hide from my oldest daughter. Keyani was not yet two years old at the time, and after I closed the door I realized I had never been in this particular closet with the door fully shut. I was a little taken back at how dark it really was in there. For several minutes I couldn't even see my hand in front of my face.

As we waited, Keyani crawled up into my lap and sat there just as content as could be. Even though I was a bit uncomfortable sitting in pitch blackness, he was not. Darkness did not intimidate him like it did me. It was almost as if he was too young and too innocent to know that people are actually afraid of the dark.

It made me wonder: Who taught us to be afraid of the dark? It wasn't a book, and it certainly wasn't the Father of Lights. It was our fallen nature, the same one that was crucified with Christ and buried in the waters of baptism. That old man is dead, so don't you dare let that dead man dictate.

Heaven is not intimidated by darkness. What seems dark to us is light to God. David writes that "the darkness and the light are both alike" to Him and that He has made "darkness His secret place" (Ps. 139:12c; 18:11). God is light and only in darkness can we truly appreciate it. Christ did not give you a torch to have you hold it up in the middle of the day. Perhaps this is why He allows darkness to surround you.

We all know the presence of ungodly fear. It is a crawling, gnawing, numbing, debilitating feeling. The way we displace this presence is with a stronger fear and a stronger presence. As terrifying as unholy fear seems in the moment, it doesn't hold a candle to standing before the Living God. Try introducing your fear to the presence of the Great King. In His presence we have no cause to fear darkness. A.W. Tozer wrote, "Outside the will of God, there's nothing I want. Inside the will of God, there's nothing I fear." Like my son in the closet, one of the ways we conquer fear is by climbing onto our Father's lap in dark times and finding security in His arms.

It is worth asking: What terrifies the devil? When God calls you to do something that terrifies you, your radical obedience is what terrifies the devil. A person walking unashamedly in the holy fear of God is Satan's greatest fear.

RUNNING FROM COURAGE

There's a story told about a man who had been plagued since childhood by a recurring dream. In his nightmare a dark image would hunt him down and chase him until he woke up exhausted and in a cold sweat. He consulted a counselor about it, and the counselor asked if he had ever confronted the image. When the man said he hadn't, the counselor suggested he try it next time he had the dream.

Not too long after, the man dreamt the dream again. As he's running, he realizes he is having this nightmare again and remembers the words of his counselor. In a moment of bravery, he turns around, points at the stalker and demands, "Who are you and  what do you want?" The dark image comes out of the shadows and says, "I'm your courage, and you've been running from me your whole life."[9]

What if the very thing we've been running from is the very thing we need? If the old adage is true—that courage is not the absence of fear but the conquest of it—then consider Psalm 91 your marching orders. Andrew Jackson said, "One man with courage makes a majority."[10]

Those who run to the secret place will also run to the battlefield. They will never have to retreat from their Big Brians again. Fear loses its stronghold when the Lord becomes our stronghold, and when we fully grasp how fearfully and wonderfully we have been made, fear can no longer hold us at gunpoint.

Boldness counteracts fear. The way to overcome fear is by doing what we are afraid to do. In other words, face your fears and do it afraid if you have to. Speak in public, witness to a stranger, open up your heart, trust another person. The trick is not to rid your stomach of butterflies but to make them fly in formation. When we confront the object of our fear, it removes the *dis* from our courage.

> *"Innumerable evils have surrounded me; my iniquities have overtaken me...therefore my heart fails me"* (Psalm 40:12).

Jesus prophesied that in the last days men's hearts will fail them due to the "fear and the expectation of those things which are coming on the earth" (Luke 21:26). Taking David's words into consideration as well, it makes you wonder if heart failure, in addition to allergies and depression, is linked to the spirit of fear. Turmoil, emotional conflict, and a broken heart take a toll on our physical hearts as well as our relationships. For us, however, this does not have to be our testimony. One of the distinguishing marks of the apocalyptic church is that we will possess divine peace in the midst of chaotic devastation.

> *"Be anxious for nothing, but in everything by prayer and supplication, with thanksgiving, let your requests be made known to God; and the peace of God, which surpasses all understanding, will guard your hearts and minds through Christ Jesus. Finally, brethren, whatever things are true, whatever things are noble, whatever things are just, whatever things are pure, whatever things are lovely, whatever things are of good report, if there is any virtue and if there is anything praiseworthy—meditate on these things"* (Philippians 4:6-8).

Anxiety is not yours to keep. Your spirit is engineered to run on a higher octane. Our attitude toward fear and anxiety should be aggressive, treating them as the threat they truly pose. Paul lays out a simple solution to anxiety disorders: Prayer and healthy thinking.

Anxiety is the consequence of a neglected prayer life or at the very least an indication of an ineffective one. It is evidence that we are worrying our prayers instead of truly casting our cares on Him. Once we lay down our burden, it is our meditation that determines our level of peace and if we ever pick that burden back up again.

THE BULLET POINT

When Christ calls us, He calls us out of cowardice. Those of faith who have walked before us were far from cowardly. They were men and women of valor and guts, possessing bravery in the midst of brutality. Their blood sounds a clarion call to our generation. Where are the bold and the courageous in our day? Where are the ones who through faith subdue kingdoms, work righteousness, obtain promises, stop the mouths of lions, quench the violence of fire, escape the edge of the sword, out of weakness are made strong, become valiant in battle, turn the flight of armies, and return to women their dead raised to life?[11]

One of the defining characteristics of the end-times will be terror. The other will be courage. Which one will define you?

ENDNOTES

1. MPAA 2011 Theatrical Market Statistics, accessed October 10, 2012, http://www.mpaa.org/Resources/5bec4ac9-a95e-443b-987b-bff6fb5455a9.pdf.

2. Filmgeeks 2.0 blog, "Theatrical Review: *The Descent*," August 12, 2006, http://darwen.us/filmgeeks/filmgeeksarchive/2006_08_01_index.html.

3. National Institute of Mental Health, accessed August 7, 2012, http://www.nimh.nih.gov/health/publications/the-numbers-count-mental-disorders-in-america/index.shtml#Anxiety.

4. "The Economic Burden of Anxiety Disorders," a study commissioned by ADAA, *The Journal of Clinical* Psychiatry 60(7), July 1999, accessed August 7, 2012, http://www.adaa.org/ about-adaa/press-room/facts-statistics.

5. The Statistics of Phobias, accessed August 7, 2012, http://intranet. micds.org/upper/health/Health-Web/vLe/Statistics_doc.html.

6. "Mental Illness: Facts and Numbers," accessed August 7, 2012, http://www.nami.org/Template.cfm?Section=About_Mental_ Illness&Template=/ContentManagement/ContentDisplay. cfm&ContentID=53155.

7. Clinical Depression Statistics, accessed August 7, 2012, http:// www.all-on-depression-help.com/clinical-depression-statistics. html.

8 A.W. Tozer, accessed October 10, 2012, https://twitter.com/ TozerAW/status/253876917638406144.

9. Based on a true story and adapted from Gordon Dalby's *Healing The Masculine Soul* (Nashville, TN: Thomas Nelson, 2003).

10. Tim Hansel, *Holy Sweat* (Dallas, TX: Word Publishing 1987), 93.

11. See Hebrews 11:33-35.

CHAPTER 8

WITH A VENGEANCE

*"A thousand may fall at your side, and ten thousand at your right hand; but it shall not come near you. Only with your eyes shall you look, and see **the reward of the wicked**"* (Psalm 91:7-8).

THE ASHES of Sodom and Gomorrah still bear witness that the kindness and severity of God is no small matter. According to biblical genealogies, these cities were populated by the descendants of Ham, one of Noah's three sons who passed through the waters of the flood. Ham brought a curse upon his son Canaan when he exposed his father's nakedness in his tent. It was this curse that the descendants of Ham sowed into the land where they settled after exiting the ark—the real estate of the Middle East. Wickedness prevailed throughout the land of Canaan for centuries until the region was eventually reclaimed and redeemed by the children of Israel in Joshua's day.

Scripture records that the outcry against Sodom and Gomorrah was so great that it reached the ears of Heaven. The Lord Himself, in the form of a man and accompanied by two angels, came down to assess the situation. After His famous conversation with Abraham, Yehovah sent the two angels disguised as men to

Sodom. When they found lodging in the house of Lot, Scripture records that all the men from the city, young and old and from every quarter, surrounded Lot's house. They demanded that the two angels be brought out so they could be immoral with them.

Sodom was a godless and depraved city, but this is not the sole reason it was destroyed. It was destroyed for its lack of a righteous remnant. We learn that if there had been only ten righteous in the city, God would have spared the wicked on behalf of the righteous. But not even ten could be found. In fact, there was barely even one.

Lot is called righteous in Scripture even though he made some very questionable decisions. He was quite willing to permit the inflamed men of Sodom to gang-rape and most likely dispose of his two virgin daughters as a concession for their demands to violate the two angels. This was eastern hospitality taken to a perverted level, to say the least. When the raging homosexual crowd refused, insisting they wanted the two strangers, the angels yanked Lot back into the house, shut the door and struck the mob with blindness. Though blind, the rowdy and determined crowd still would not relent, wearing themselves out to fulfill their lusts as they groped to find the door.

Vexed and armed with the fury of Heaven, the angels urgently warned Lot to flee from the coming wrath of God, but Lot was still reluctant. The angels had to physically grab him and his family and escort them to the gates of the city. When Lot continued to resist and complained that escaping to the mountains was too dangerous, the angels showed him mercy and allowed them to flee to the nearby city of Zoar.

Peter writes that God "rescued Lot out of Sodom because he was a righteous man who was sick of all the shameful immorality of the wicked people around him. Yes, Lot was a righteous man who was tormented in his soul by the wickedness he saw and heard day after day. So you see, the Lord knows how to rescue godly people from their trials, even while keeping the wicked under punishment until the day of final judgment" (2 Pet. 2:7-9 NLT).

Scripture regards Lot as righteous, even though his actions appear suspect. He was the only righteous one in all of Sodom, perhaps even the only righteous person in his own family. Lot's wife disregarded the orders of the angels and looked back. She immediately turned into a salt lick. Some time later, Lot's daughters hatched a plan to get impregnated by their father. On what must have been some very strong wine, they got Lot drunk on two successive evenings and slept with him. The plan worked, and they both conceived. One bore a son named Moab; the other bore a son named Ammon. Both proved to be painful thorns in the side of the Israelites for generations to come.

God displayed extreme kindness to a man with questionable morals. Perhaps there was enough good in Lot to activate God's mercy. Scripture, however, says that the mercy extended toward Lot was on account of Abraham, who was Lot's uncle. Moses writes that "when God destroyed the cities of the plain, that God remembered Abraham, and sent Lot out of the midst of the overthrow, when He overthrew the cities in which Lot had dwelt" (Gen. 19:29).

Lot was righteous, but not righteous like Abraham. Abraham was a man of unusual faith—faith that produced righteousness. Because of his righteousness and because of Abraham's relationship with Yehovah, the Lord spared Abraham's compromising family from judgment. When God sought a man who might stand in the gap for Sodom, He didn't turn to Lot. He turned to Abraham, and this was not the first time Abraham had to rescue Lot. Arthur Wallis writes, "Abraham did far more for Sodom from without than Lot ever did from within."[1]

Let this encourage us as well. As we seek to make the Righteous One our refuge, He is willing and kind to spare our loved ones for our sake. His mercy to them is His mercy extended toward us, and the favor we gain with Him in the secret place can also gain protection for our families as well.

The notion that our churches must move into the ghetto, buy up real estate and occupy the dens of iniquity in order to reach the city doesn't hold up here. Not that there

> "In every generation the number of the righteous is small. Be sure you are among them."[2] A.W. Tozer

is anything wrong with having a presence in our inner cities, but Abraham did from his home what Lot was unable to do from within the city. The key is not influence with man, but influence with God, and this is what Psalm 91 secures for us.

SALT CONTENT

Righteousness expressed through right actions is a refuge. It has the ability to stay the judgment of God on our lives, families and the land in which we live. Our concern should not only be with the level of wickedness in our communities but also with the condition and state of the children of light. Any judgment placed on our city is an indictment against us as well. We should take it personally when the Consuming Fire judges our nation, for "the time has come for judgment to begin at the house of God; and if it begins with us first, what will be the end of those who do not obey the gospel of God?" (1 Pet. 4:17).

Perhaps our salt content is to blame for the collapse of our nation's morals. Is it possible that Lot's wife turned into a pillar of salt outside of the city because she had ceased to be salt within it? Any eroded shield of protection over a country has happened on our watch and can be pointed back to our ranks. If those who are called to be a righteous remnant are no longer righteous, then we can no longer be considered the remnant. Our fate then will be tied to the fate of the wicked. A.W. Tozer said, "In every generation the number of the righteous is small. Be sure you are among them."[3]

The God of Heaven and Earth is gracious and compassionate, slow to anger, rich in love. He is a Holy God, a Loving Father, a Sovereign Ruler, a Faithful Friend, a Glorious King, a Mighty Warrior, a Jealous Husband, and a Strong Deliverer. But He is also a Righteous Judge, and He still judges nations and cities and families and people. It is and will always be "a fearful thing to fall into the hands of the living God" (Heb. 10:31).

His incredible patience with sinners still always amazes me. He gives all a lifetime to repent, but we should not take His long-suffering for granted or mistake it for indifference. Just because He doesn't pay at the end of the week doesn't mean He doesn't pay.

LOVE AND FURY

There's a story told about a boy who was drowning in a lake and cried out to a man passing by. The man jumped into the water and rescued him from death. Some time later, this boy was caught stealing and brought to court. The very man who had saved him that day at the lake was the judge sitting on the bench. "Surely," the boy thought, "this man will save me. I am safe." After hearing the case, the judge declared him guilty and sentenced him. The boy blurted out, "But you were the man who saved me." The judge replied, "Young man, one day I was your savior, but today I am your judge."

God is loving by desire but judging by necessity. Some characterize Him as angry in the Old Testament and merciful in the New, but this is an inaccurate portrayal in my estimation. He is loving in both the Old and the New. He was just as loving when raining down sulfur on Sodom as when He released the woman caught in adultery. He was loving when He evicted the Canaanites from the Promised Land, and He was loving when He healed the paralytic. All of His actions are loving, even His judgments. When that doesn't seem to be the case, it means our definition of love is skewed and needs to be redefined. We need to look no further than God's every move to find the true essence of love.

Love heals and love forgives. Love carries the cross and forgives its enemies. But love also stands up to cruelty and fights for the object of its affection. Our God is both a perfect Lover and a perfect Judge, and His loving nature is not inconsistent with His vengeance. In fact, He could not be a lover if He did not defend His holiness and act on behalf of the innocent, the poor, and the disadvantaged.

Some question how a loving God could destroy an entire city or expel a people group from a region, but what about the countless atrocities committed in those cities or regions? Is there no justice for the innocent?

Like a just judge He must punish evildoers, and like a good shepherd He delights in warding off predators that threaten the sheep. There is love in His fury because it is love that fuels His passion and rouses Him to fight for our hearts. It's not that the Avenger ceases to love when He punishes; it's that His love demands an active response to injustice.

Perhaps a definition of the wrath of God is necessary here. When I speak of wrath, I do not mean it is when God loses His temper. I don't get the sense that He feels personally slighted by someone's disobedience to His will. Neither is His wrath a fit of rage or an outburst of anger. His wrath is simply His hostility toward sin and His protection of the pure in heart. It's when holiness meets heartlessness, when justice squashes tyranny, when truth exposes lies, and when good triumphs over evil.

The rainbow is a great example of God's loving wrath. It reminds us of His promise to creation as well as His judgment of it. It is both a sign of covenant and a sign of warning, a sober reminder of what we are capable of if given over to moral depravity. The rainbow then serves a dual purpose—to comfort and to caution. God will never destroy the earth again using floodwaters, but considering the many different ways our planet could be destroyed, that may not be too reassuring.

It's ironic that the homosexual community has adopted the rainbow to represent their sinful lifestyle. In light of Sodom, Gomorrah and the flood, their movement is no more secure than a house of cards built on a fault line. Little do they realize that all of their rainbow bumper stickers and t-shirts are prophesying to them. Next time you see a rainbow, let it serve as a reminder that our Maker is covenant-keeping God whose holiness demands our careful and close consideration.

PROGRESSION OF IMMORALITY

God's wrath does not always look like Sodom and Gomorrah. In fact, His judgment is generally not of the fire and brimstone variety. Romans chapter 1 outlines how a society spirals downward into self-destructive, moral bankruptcy.

"For the wrath of God is revealed from heaven against all ungodliness and unrighteousness of men, who suppress the truth in unrighteousness, because what may be known of God is manifest in them, for God has shown it to them. For since the creation of the world His invisible attributes are clearly seen, being understood by the things that are made, even His eternal power and Godhead, so that they are without excuse, because, although they knew God, they did not glorify Him as God, nor were thankful, but became futile in their thoughts, and their foolish hearts were darkened. Professing to be wise, they became fools, and changed the glory of the incorruptible God into an image made like corruptible man—and birds and four-footed animals and creeping things. Therefore God also gave them up to uncleanness, in the lusts of their hearts, to dishonor their bodies among themselves, who exchanged the truth of God for the lie, and worshiped and served the creature rather than the Creator, who is blessed forever. Amen. For this reason God gave them up to vile passions. For even their women exchanged the natural use for what is against nature. Likewise also the men, leaving the natural use of the woman, burned in their lust for one another, men with men committing what is shameful, and receiving in themselves the penalty of their error which was due. And even as they did not like to retain God in their knowledge, God gave them over to a debased mind, to do those things which are not fitting; being filled with all unrighteousness, sexual immorality, wickedness, covetousness, maliciousness; full of envy, murder, strife, deceit, evil-mindedness; they are whisperers, backbiters, haters of God, violent, proud, boasters, inventors of evil things, disobedient to parents, undiscerning, untrustworthy, unloving, unforgiving, unmerciful; who, knowing the righteous judgment of God, that those who practice such things are deserving of death, not only do the same but also approve of those who practice them" (Romans 1:18-32).

This is the progression of sin in a society that rebels against its Maker.

1. **Suffocation of truth**—"For the wrath of God is revealed from heaven against all...who suppress the truth in unrighteousness" (v. 18).

2. **Indifference to worship**—"Although they knew God, they did not glorify Him as God, nor were thankful..." (v. 21).

3. **Senseless thinking**—"...Became futile in their thoughts, and their foolish hearts were darkened. Professing to be wise, they became fools" (vv. 21-22).

4. **Replacement of God**—"Changed the glory of the incorruptible God into an image made like corruptible man..." (v. 23).

5. **Idolizing creation**—"...Birds and four-footed animals and creeping things.... who exchanged the truth of God for the lie, and worshiped and served the creature rather than the Creator..." (vv. 23, 25).

6. **Corruption of heart**—"God also gave them up to uncleanness, in the lusts of their hearts, to dishonor their bodies among themselves" (v. 24).

7. **Perverse affections**—"...God gave them up to vile passions. For even their women exchanged the natural use for what is against nature. Likewise also the men, leaving the natural use of the woman, burned in their lust for one another, men with men committing what is shameful..." (vv. 26-27).

8. **Celebration of evil**—"Being filled with all unrighteousness, sexual immorality, wickedness, covetousness, maliciousness; full of envy, murder, strife, deceit, evil-mindedness; they are whisperers, backbiters, haters of God, violent, proud, boasters, inventors of evil things, disobedient to parents,

undiscerning, untrustworthy, unloving, unforgiving, unmerciful; who, knowing the righteous judgment of God, that those who practice such things are deserving of death, not only do the same but also approve of those who practice them" (vv. 29-32).

The final stage of moral collapse is a total reversal of values. A society is on the verge of implosion when it celebrates evil and reviles righteousness, when its heroes are vile and its enemies are virtuous, when immorality is praised and purity is despised. Isaiah warns, "Woe to those who call evil good, and good evil; who put darkness for light, and light for darkness; who put bitter for sweet, and sweet for bitter!" (Is. 5:20).

Paul repeats that the Judge of the Earth "gave them up" and "gave them over" to the consequences of their actions (Rom. 1:24, 26, 28). Humanity always loses itself when it loses sight of its Maker, and the moment people turn away from the Source of Life is the moment death settles in. The natural course of sin is extinction, and eventually mankind will destroy itself if left to its own devices. Letting mankind reap what it sows is the simplest form of God's judgment.

Humanity always loses itself when it loses sight of its Maker.

COULD SODOM EVER HAPPEN AGAIN?

During the two-day volcanic eruption of Mount Vesuvius, the first-century towns of Pompeii and Herculaneum were completely obliterated and nearly forgotten for almost 1600 years. Buried under thousands of tons of volcanic ash piled seventy feet high, the ruins of Pompeii were discovered accidentally in 1599 by Italian engineer Domenico Fontana while working on a hydraulics project. However, archaeologists did not begin to unearth the city until around 1748.

A resort town estimated at 12,000 to 20,000 citizens, the ancient city of Pompeii was home to the aristocracy of the Roman Empire. It boasted of grand public buildings, spacious gardens, elaborate houses, central heating, hot baths, a vast sports arena, two theatres, fresh water supply, swimming pools, and no fewer than eighty-nine fast-food cafés. Not far away was the famed Villa Oplontis, an elaborate hundred-room villa of Poppaea Sabina, the mistress and eventual second wife of Nero. Like Poppaea, the Roman Empire had a notorious reputation for sexual promiscuity. Sex with both genders and all ages was welcomed and considered a gift to the gods. In return, these gods gave them sexually transmitted diseases. Not a very good trade-off.

Archaeologists reveal that in the early afternoon of August, AD 79, people were going about their daily routine—some at work, some taking baths, some trading in the market. Those who weren't working were gathered in Rome's oldest amphitheatre for the summer games. When Vesuvius blew and a twenty-mile high column of ash blasted out from the mountain, at least half of the city's population was not present to witness it. A large group of citizens had already fled the city, having been spooked by a sizable earthquake that struck days before the eruption.

In addition to the earthquake, there were other warning signs leading up to its eruption—springs stopping, wells drying up and birds ceasing to sing. Even stray dogs were observed walking for a day and half in the hot summer sun to escape the coming danger.[4]

Those who remained were caught off guard. Some were trampled to death; others were killed by flying volcanic debris. The final wave of devastation was a pyroclastic flow that surged down the sides of the mountain at speeds of over 300 miles per hour and at temperatures of 400 degrees Fahrenheit. These superheated gases destroyed everything and everyone in its path. Within four days, the entire city of Pompeii was engulfed and buried in burning ash and pumice.

I watched a documentary about Pompeii on the Discovery Channel, and it told the story of fifty-four men, women and children who found refuge in a cellar. Their skeletons reveal what life might have been like in their final moments. One woman was pregnant while another man was of African descent. There were twin sisters who had congenital syphilis, as well as a very rich man whose bones were stained green from his jewelry.

What caught the attention of the archaeologists was that there were two noticeable groups huddled together on separate sides of the room. One group was found with nothing but their skeletons. The other group died with cash, gold and jewels of all kinds. Even in their death, the rich clung to their property and possessions. These fifty-four souls might have initially survived the flying pumice and the pyroclastic surge but most likely died of thermal shock not long into the night. Their helpless refuge was only sufficient enough to extend their lives by a few hours.[5]

What stands out to me is that the destruction of Pompeii is not too different from the destruction of Sodom. Both cities were wicked. Both were notoriously immoral. Both were destroyed by fire and heat, and the exact location of both of these cities had been kept hidden for hundreds of years. In each case, warning signs and a way of escape were offered and provided. Considering the unchangeable nature of our God, to think that something like this could never happen again in our time is ignorant and perhaps even arrogant.

For you and me, however, an evacuation route has already been mapped out. Christ is God's provision for our escape. The God of grace ordains the terrors of His wrath and the tenderness of His mercy to draw us to salvation. Even for wicked Sodom and for the inhabitants of Pompeii, a way of escape was provided for those who had ears to hear.

JUDGMENT: NOW OR LATER

"Man is destined to die once, and after that to face judgment" (Hebrews 9:27 NIV).

"For if we would judge ourselves, we would not be judged. But when we are judged, we are chastened by the Lord, that we may not be condemned with the world" (1 Corinthians 11:31-32).

My constant prayer is that Christ would judge me now and expose my hidden sin on this side of eternity, so that I will not be condemned for it on the other side of eternity. The more we allow the Righteous Judge to examine our lives now, the better chance of gaining a favorable outcome when our lives are over. Judgment now is far better than judgment later, and it is His mercy that our sin be exposed while still living than when standing before His throne. At least now we have the opportunity to repent and change our ways.

Jesus is the great lifeguard of life. He jumped into the waters of humanity to save us from drowning in our sin. There is one person, however, whom no lifeguard can save. It's the person trying to save himself. One of the sad tragedies and horrors of Judgment Day will be that a life preserver was thrown, available and within reach by those who stand condemned, but they refused it because they thought they could save themselves.

DODGING BULLETS

On the day that our country celebrated its Bicentennial, another nation celebrated a stunning triumph of freedom. In June of 1976, four hijackers forced an Air France plane carrying 248 passengers to land at Entebbe Airport in Uganda. Joining forces with local terrorists and soldiers, the hijackers released all the non-Jewish passengers and crew, but held 105 Jewish and Israeli passengers hostage.

As members of the German Revolutionary Cells and the Popular Front for the Liberation of Palestine, the terrorists quickly gave their terms and demanded the release of fifty-three convicted terrorists imprisoned in Israel. Despite several rounds of negotiations, the hijackers issued an ultimatum. If their demands were not met by 1 p.m. on July 4th, they would start executing hostages.

Faced with few options, the Israeli government entered into negotiations to buy time, giving the Israel Defense Forces (IDF) an entire week to come up with a plan. On July 3 they flew two hundred of their top Special Forces 2,500 miles in stealth to carry out a daring raid of the airport. Heavily armed and using the element of surprise, the soldiers stormed the terminal and freed the hostages, killing all guerrilla forces as well as forty-five Ugandan soldiers in the process. After traveling for half a day, the entire raid of the airport from touchdown to takeoff took only fifty-eight minutes.

When the Israeli troops entered the terminal, they shouted in Hebrew, "Get down. Crawl." The Hebrew-speaking hostages understood and dropped to the floor as bullets sprayed the room. Two hostages hesitated and were caught in the crossfire. Another was lying down when the commandos stormed the airport but stood up to his death. Had these three heeded the soldiers' commands, they would have been freed with the rest of the captives. Unfortunately, the bullets meant for their captors led to their demise.

Due to the risk, distance traveled and casualty-to-hostage ratio, the Entebbe rescue is widely considered one of the most bold and successful counterterrorist missions in history. Named Operation Thunderbolt, it is also referred to as Operation Jonathan in memory of force commander Yonatan Netanyahu, who was tragically killed while leading hostages safely toward rescue aircraft. Jonathan was the older brother of Prime Minster Benjamin Netanyahu.[6]

THE BULLET POINT

The bullets of God's wrath are for your freedom, not for your destruction. They are for your enemies, not for you. In Christ, we automatically dodge the biggest bullet of all—eternal damnation. Like these freedom fighters, the heavenly Father ran a rescue mission when He sent His Force Commander to sacrifice His life to set the captives free. The key to our liberation is to heed His words and get low enough to humble ourselves. "God opposes the proud but gives grace to the humble" (James 4:6b NIV). Without humility, we always find ourselves on the wrong side of the opposition, and the bullets meant to protect may actually destroy us. So long as we stay close to Him, the Avenger's vengeance will be our vindication instead of our destruction.

ENDNOTES

1. Arthur Wallis, *In the Day of Thy Power* (Colombia, MO: Cityhill Publishing and Fort Washington, PA: Christian Literature Crusade, 1990), 129.

2 A.W. Tozer, *The Root Of Righteousness* (1955), Introduction.

3. A.W. Tozer, *The Root of the Righteous*, accessed August 7, 2012, http://www.scribd.com/doc/32207711/THE-ROOT-OF-THE-RIGHTEOUS-A-W-TOZER-1955.

4. "The Real Dogs of Pompeii," accessed August 7, 2912, http://www.dogsofpompeii.com/tour.php.

5. *Pompeii: Back From the Dead*, narrated by Don Wildman, Discovery Channel documentary, Season 2011, Episode 8, aired April 18, 2011.

6. Craig Brian Larson, *Illustrations for Preaching & Teaching* (Grand Rapids, MI: Baker Books, 1993), 157; "The Entebbe Rescue Mission," accessed August 7, 2012, http://www.jewishvirtuallibrary.org/jsource/Terrorism/entebbe.html.

CHAPTER 9

REFUGEES & PREPPERS

*"Because you have made the LORD, who is **my refuge**, even the Most High, your dwelling place, no evil shall befall you, nor shall any plague come near your dwelling"* (Psalm 91:9-10).

THE PROPHECIES have been circulating now for several years, warnings of earthquakes, riots, superstorms, epidemics, economic disaster, energy shortages, and earth-shattering calamities. Some words are vague and self-evident like increases in crime and conflict in the Middle East. Others are more specific like tap water becoming more expensive than oil and Las Vegas being reduced to a ghost town.

In the wave of prophecies directed our way, a handful mention California. This caught our attention since we live near Napa Valley in Northern California. One minister dreamt of a major earthquake splitting San Francisco in two, leaving half the city underwater. Another saw the Golden Gate Bridge crumble and crash into the Bay. One famous prophet proclaimed that Los Angeles would one day lie at the bottom of the ocean.

John Paul Jackson's word about a ten-year perfect storm coming to America has been in circulation since 2008. In it he speaks of food scarcity, city evacuations, grocery stores emptied in an hour, blight devastating hybrid seeds, people frantically digging up pavement to plant crops, abandoned shopping malls doubling as temporary housing, nuclear material smuggled into the U.S. through underground tunnels, an assassination attempt on the president, Israel bombing Iran, tornadoes carrying 350-mph winds, a dirty bomb exploding in a coastal city and the rise of anti-Semitism due to soaring fuel costs.

He saw the year 2010 growing more difficult as it progressed and heard the voice of an angel emphatically say three times, "The woes of 2012." Although some of these predictions may seem plausible today, they weren't in 2008. Given the state of the world's economy, scenarios such as food shortages, abandoned shopping malls and soaring energy costs are no longer far-fetched.

When we were made aware of these words, Meljoné and I were unsure how seriously to take these kinds of warnings. On one hand, if accurate, this is serious business. Words of prophecy are not something to be taken lightly, and we have no intention of turning a deaf ear to the voice of God. On the other hand, quite a number of widely believed doom-and-gloom prophecies have never come to pass. Who are the ones prophesying these events? Are they accurate or misguided? Is God bringing judgment of this magnitude to our land?

As we discussed this topic with other believers, we were met with strong opinions and varying degrees of emotion—fear, skepticism, hope and indifference. For us and for our community of believers, it gave us incentive to run to the secret place and find out for ourselves. As we did, the Lord began to speak—and in surprising fashion.

Through a series of dreams, pictures and prophetic directives, we felt the Holy Spirit was asking us and our community to prepare.[1] What exactly we were to prepare for was uncertain, but we thought it prudent to prepare ourselves in tangible ways even without knowing what we were preparing for. That meant being physically, spiritually, emotionally, and financially sober, ready and alert. That meant shoring up our finances and changing our spending habits. It meant having our car in good working order. It meant buying extra food, water, blankets, and duct tape periodically on trips to the store. No scenario was unreasonable or out of bounds for us.

At times Meljoné and I would look at each other and say, "Are we crazy to be doing this?", but it never felt awkward to our spirits. Solomon writes, "A prudent man foresees evil and hides himself, but the simple pass on and are punished" (Prov. 22:3; see also 27:12). Even without a prophetic tip-off, having an emergency escape plan and extra supplies on hand is sensible. If you live in earthquake country as we do or in an area susceptible to natural disasters, stocking up on emergency supplies is recommended and never a bad idea.

We quickly learned that there is a term for this kind of extreme behavior. We've come to grips with the fact that we might be labeled by some as, dare I say, preppers!

PREPPERS

You don't need me to inform you that the prepper movement is in full swing. From weekend warriors to soccer moms, from doomsayers to intercessors this is not your father's survivalist. Complete with survival shows, canning techniques, underground bunkers, ammunition networks, emergency food suppliers, disaster preparation courses, websites, and reality TV shows, survivalism has arrived. No longer is the movement marginalized by antigovernment conspiracy theorists hiding out in some mountain bunker awaiting and perhaps secretly hoping for the apocalypse. What began with the out-of-touch lunatic fringe has grown into a populace of concerned citizens attempting to take their survival into their own hands. Not surprisingly, it has also developed into an enormous money-making industry.

Modern preppers are not easy to identify simply because most are average people living normal lives. For one reason or another, preppers feel the need to store up resources to protect and provide for their families in the event of cataclysmic catastrophe. What they are preparing for is varied and wide. For some it's economic disaster or natural calamity; for others it's war or nuclear radiation, but what fuels them is a compelling attraction to and urgency for self-sufficency.

In some ways, Noah could be considered a prepper. He lived in a time when the whole earth was utterly corrupt and full of violence. So great was man's wickedness that God was grieved and even sorry He had created man, but Noah found favor. Following very specific blueprints for a boat made of gopherwood, Noah's faith and obedience led to the preservation of life on earth. What is often lost in the story of Noah is his fortitude. Many scholars believe it took 120 years to complete the ark from start to finish.

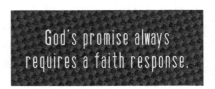

God's promise always requires a faith response.

One might call Joseph a prepper. He interpreted Pharaoh's dream of a coming famine correctly and wisely stored up grain in the times of plenty to serve as storehouses in the times of lack. Although it wasn't a 120-year project, Joseph personally oversaw the food storage/distribution operation and saw the revelation through for fourteen years.

Even Paul the apostle had prepper tendencies. When Agabus stood up and foretold that a great famine was coming, the disciples in Antioch took up a collection for the Jerusalem community and sent it by way of Paul and Barnabas. These two apostles carried with them a rather large sum of money all the way to Jerusalem for the purpose of famine relief. History confirms that the predicted famine did indeed come to Judea in AD 44 just as Agabus had prophesied. It lasted three years and affected the entire region of Judea as well as the Phoenician coast. Josephus records that this famine was so severe that many people died of starvation due to the extreme scarcity and expense of food.[2]

In each of these cases, God's protection integrated man's cooperation. For these men of faith, remaining passive and expecting God to intervene just because they were given a word of the Lord or had gained His favor was not quite adequate. They acted upon the revelation, understanding that God's promise always requires a faith response.

We all could be considered preppers in one way or another. College savings, health insurance, spare tires, storm drains, rainy day funds, wedding planners, fire extinguishers, retirement accounts—preparing for the future is a way of life, even for believers. After all, isn't this age merely a dress rehearsal for the age to come? Every season of life is designed to prepare us for the next season of life.

Although one may not be inclined to prepare to the extent that another does, the call to prepare ourselves for prophetic events such as the coming of the Bridegroom is unquestioned and universal in Scripture. Keep in mind that the books of Daniel, Revelation, and the Prophets were not written merely for knowledge or informational value. They were written so that we could detect the signs of the times and prepare ourselves and the world for what lies ahead. In this way, wisdom and preparation go hand in hand.

PREPARING BY FAITH

"Prepare the way of the LORD..." (Isaiah 40:3b).

"And that servant who knew his master's will, and did not prepare himself or do according to his will, shall be beaten with many stripes.." (Luke 12:47).

There is a fundamental difference between those who prepare from a posture of fear and those who prepare from a posture of faith. Those in fear feverishly squirrel away provisions trying to insulate themselves from loss or lack. They are too easily caught up in the paranoia of uncertainty and what might could possibly maybe happen someday. This is the servant who buried his talent. This is the rich man who tore down his barns to build bigger ones. Self-preservation makes people do wacky things, and those who are motivated by it are fooled into believing that it's their preparation that will save them from danger, real or perceived.

Those who prepare by faith, however, are caught up in the pulses of Heaven. Like Noah, Joseph and the disciples of Antioch, they prepare in response to a word from Heaven. Their motivation is not self-preservation but rather concern for the poor, the widowed, the orphaned, and for all those they are called to protect. They realize that their preparation is not their salvation, but that salvation comes from the One who knows the future and has instructed them to prepare.

Preparedness is not a reliable refuge in itself. Without an accompanied faith in the Savior, it is as useless as a life preserver made of cement. Any motivation for preparation must be accompanied with reliance upon the One who gives and preserves life. Being prepared is not a lack of faith, but relying on that preparation to save you is.

This is why a person's motivation for preparation is so vital and telling. A good number of preppers probably do prepare from a place of common sense and wisdom, but there are some who are preparing out of panic and self-interest. For a believer, this is never the right motive. Our focus should not be self-reliance and self-preservation. It should always be God-reliance and self-sacrifice.

For Noah, Joseph and the early church, their insight into the future did not come from the internet, *60 Minutes* or The Weather Channel. It came from Heaven. Their preparation was not in response to the fear of loss but rather the fear of the Lord. They put their faith into action, trusting in God's provision and protection as they prepared, even putting their own safety and reputation at risk to save those around them.

It should be no different for us. I have come to realize that my existence is not and has never been in my own hands. My survival belongs to the Sustainer of my soul. Any preparation that I have saved up or secured is not so much for my sake but for those around me who may find themselves unprepared and without God's provision or protection.

RAPTURE & THE END-TIMES

Theology plays a larger role in the discussion of preparation than one might realize. The idea of preparation seems pointless and a waste of time to those who interpret from the Scriptures that God will rapture the church before the days of tribulation. From this point of view, Christians leave behind a world on a collision course with destruction while they safely watch from the sidelines of Heaven. It makes sense. Why prepare for something we won't be around to witness?

I once held this viewpoint but have since changed my eschatology. I'm convinced the church is present and active throughout the book of Revelation and will be a force to be reckoned with during the Great Tribulation. This perspective is not without biblical precedent. God did not choose to remove Noah from the planet when the floodwaters arose. The Israelites lived in Egypt and were shielded from the plagues. Rahab remained in the city in the midst of its destruction. Jeremiah lived through and survived Babylonian captivity.

For some, the rapture solves the problem of how the Bride of Christ is preserved during the days of wrath, but God does not have to rapture us to protect us. He is more than capable of sustaining His people in the midst of His judgments, as is His biblical pattern. If it is our safety that concerns us and dictates our eschatology, perhaps this is why we've been given Psalm 91.

Goshen is no less glorious than being instantly transported to paradise. The house of Rahab is as effective of a refuge as is a rapture. Whether the fiery furnace, Red Sea, lion's den, city of Pella, or belly of a whale, the safest place in the universe is being in the center of God's will. We need not fear the events of the end-times so long as our soul is hidden in the secret place.

WILLING TO GO, PREPARING TO STAY

Whether before or after the tribulation, the second coming of Christ will not come as a surprise for those who keep in step with the Spirit. Jesus spoke of wars, rumors of wars, famines, pestilence, and earthquakes occurring in the last days.[3] He said this:

> *"For as in the days before the flood, they were eating and drinking, marrying and giving in marriage, until the day that Noah entered the ark, and did not know until the flood came and took them all away, so also will the coming of the Son of Man be. Then*

two men will be in the field: one will be taken and the other left. Two women will be grinding at the mill: one will be taken and the other left. Watch therefore, for you do not know what hour your Lord is coming" (Matthew 24:38-42).

The one taken is not a reference to the rapture. It speaks of His second coming and the hour of His judgment. These are simultaneous events. This explains why Jesus uses the example of Noah here. One will be kept safe from the flood of destruction while another is swept away in it. One will enter the ark of God's protection while the other is left outside. Those who are watchful may not know the day or the hour of His coming, but I'm confident they will know the times and the season.

"By faith Noah, being divinely warned of things not yet seen, moved with godly fear, prepared an ark for the saving of his household..." (Hebrews 11:7).

Noah entered the ark by faith, just as Jochebed placed Moses in the basket. Likewise, so must we. Just as our spiritual salvation requires faith, so does our physical salvation.

I've learned that it's counterproductive and a sign of insecurity to remain dogmatic about end-time events. Because the knowledge of God is fluid, so too should our theology be, which is why I try to hold my eschatological opinions loosely.

If I am appointed to live at the time of the Great Tribulation, I have every intention of sticking around and rescuing as many souls possible for the Kingdom of Heaven. I'm ready for the persecution that comes with it. I'm prepared to lay down my life. If the gathering of the saints occurs before the seals, trumpets and bowls, I won't go kicking and screaming. I'm planning to stay but quite willing to go despite my theology.

But if the church is ordained to stand and be present in the midst of those troubling times, what of those who are expecting to go and not planning to stay?

They will be left physically, emotionally, spiritually, and financially shell-shocked and ill-equipped for the adversity of those times. They've banked their future on a doctrine that, if wrong, leaves them dangerously unprepared. For this reason alone we should not discount those among us who feel inclined to prep.

It was Ralph Waldo Emerson who famously said, "The future belongs to those who prepare for it."[4] Because Bible-believing saints are privy to insider information about the future of the earth, we should have a corner on the apocalypse market. We alone know the ultimate fate of our planet.

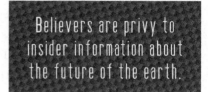

Believers are privy to insider information about the future of the earth.

PRACTICAL GUIDELINES FOR PREPARATION

Here are some of the challenges that the church will face in this coming hour as well as some essentials for faith preparation.

Water

Water is the basic building block of life and the most important commodity on earth. It existed before the account of creation, as it is written, "…darkness was on the face of the deep. And the Spirit of God was hovering over the face of the waters" (Gen. 1:2). A person can live for a long time without food but not more than three or four days without water. This is why ancient civilizations built cities in close proximity to a fresh water source.

When we turn on the faucet we take for granted that water will come out. However, it really doesn't take much to interrupt that flow or to affect the quality of the water piped into our homes. John foresaw a day when fresh water supplies on earth would be contaminated not once but twice.

> *"Then the third angel sounded: And a great star fell from heaven, burning like a torch, and it fell on a third of the rivers and on the springs of water. The name of the star is Wormwood. A third*

of the waters became wormwood, and many men died from the water, because it was made bitter" (Revelation 8:10-11).

"Then the third angel poured out his bowl on the rivers and springs of water, and they became blood" (Revelation 16:4).

Contaminated water is not beyond God's ability to heal. He healed the bitter waters of Marah by having Moses throw a tree branch into the waters. Likewise, Elisha healed the unpleasant waters of Jericho by casting a bowl of salt into its source. Jesus went even a step further. He turned bath water into fine wine for all the wedding guests at Cana.

The issue of God's miraculous ability to provide clean drinking water for us is not in question. What is in question is our tendency toward miraculous presumption. Expecting God to perform a miracle when it's in our power to take action is spiritual conjecture and ill-advised. That's like pulling into the gas station after realizing you forgot your wallet and insisting God supernaturally fill your tank just because you don't want the hassle of returning home to retrieve it. We must be careful not to confuse laziness and irresponsibility with faith.

There's a Chinese proverb that says, "Is it not already too late if one waits until one is thirsty to begin digging a well?"[5] Digging a well can be just as spiritual as throwing a healing twig into the water, as long as it is God's provision. Those who by faith feel led to store water in their garage for their households are no more extreme than those who don't. In fact, given our dire dependency on water to sustain life, perhaps the extreme ones are those who don't.

To those inclined toward preparatory action, you might consider purchasing a portable water purifier in addition to having a two-week supply of drinking water on hand. This can mobilize you and help provide fresh, clean drinking water for yourself and those around you. In the event of a water shortage in your home, filling up a bathtub, sink and any other containers with water can serve as short-term potable water supplies. Remember also that pipes, toilet tanks, and water heaters are useful reservoirs of water right in your own residence.

Food

If you haven't noticed, food prices are skyrocketing. While water is the most important commodity to store, food is the most complex. It is best to have a system in order. Root cellars are wonderful, but freezers and food storage systems are great options for those limited in space. If you feel you must, find foods that preserve well. Oxygen absorbers and bay leaves come in handy when storing food long-term, and be sure to rotate your reserve by eating what expires first.

Like water, the supernatural provision of food is not uncommon in Scripture. Quail covered the camp and manna fell from the sky for the Israelites in the desert. The widow's oil refused to run dry. Ravens, like waitresses on roller skates, brought out food to Elijah at Cherith. Elisha purified a poisonous pot of stew during a famine, and then supernaturally fed a hundred men on meager rations. Who can forget when Jesus multiplied the food and ordered fish sandwiches for everybody? This happened not once but twice!

Mel Tari, a young man during the famed Indonesian revival, tells an entertaining story of food multiplication in his book *Like a Mighty Wind*.

"Another special miracle took place when the very first team went out to preach the Gospel. They came to a small village called Nikiniki. As is the custom, the team went to the pastor's house to stay with him. The pastor happened to be my uncle. My aunt, the pastor's wife, was embarrassed because so many people came and she had nothing to give them to eat. It was famine time in Timor.

"The Lord spoke to the leader of the team, and he went to my aunt and said, 'Ma'am, the Lord told me that you have four tapioca roots in your cupboard and that you should take them and cook them. They will be sufficient for all of us.'

"'How do you know that I have four tapioca roots?' she asked.

"'I didn't know; the Lord told me,' he replied.

"She went to the kitchen and found exactly four roots as the Lord had revealed to the team member. After she had cooked the tapioca, the team leader said, 'Please get water for tea.'

"My aunt had enough sugar and tea for only two or three cups, but she obeyed. 'Put the water, tea and sugar in the pitcher and mix it up for the people to drink as they eat the tapioca,' the leader said. She did as he told her. Then she made a small flat loaf of bread out of the tapioca, put it on a plate and prayed over it. The team leader also prayed. After they prayed, the Lord told them to give each of the guests a plate, which they did. They also handed out cups.

"Then the Lord said to the team member, 'Now tell the pastor's wife that she is to break the tapioca into pieces and give it to the people until their plates are full.' Even though she thought, 'This is impossible to do, because there isn't enough to fill one plate,' she obeyed the Lord.

"The first man who came for food was pretty glad. 'If I am at the first of the line, I'll be sure to eat,' he thought. But the man who was last in line, who was a real good friend of mine, was quite upset because he liked to eat a lot. He was a big guy. I asked him later, 'What did you feel at the time?' He said, 'I was really scared. I prayed real hard and said, "Lord, I'm the last one in the line. There is only one tapioca loaf. Only three or four will have any. So, Lord Jesus, you had better perform a miracle, and please remember me, who's the last one in line, because I'm really hungry."'

"My aunt then took the bread and broke it. Usually mathematics will tell you that when you break one in half, you get two halves. This is not necessarily so in God's counting. My aunt broke one, and then the half in her right hand became whole again. The Lord told her to put the one that was in her left hand on the plate. She broke the one in her right hand again, and as she did this, it made her cry because she realized that a miracle was taking place in her hand. So she just praised the Lord and cried and broke the bread.

"The first man had a plateful and the second one, and the third one. Now everyone realized that a miracle was taking place. Even my friend who was the last one in line got a plateful. He too thanked the Lord and said, 'Oh, Lord, You've done a miracle.'

"All of them, after they had eaten some tapioca bread, came for tea at the same time. When you eat tapioca it is so dry, if you don't get something to drink you feel terrible. My aunt wanted to put only a little bit in the cups, but the Lord said, 'Just fill the cups up.' She obeyed again, and the tea just kept coming until all of them had something to drink. Many of them had two or three glasses of tea. So all of the team ate until they were completely full.

"As a matter of fact, there was enough food left over they couldn't eat. So even the dogs were satisfied; the Lord even took care of the animals."[6]

As we approach the end of the age, I believe we also approach the age of miracles. The multiplication of food will become commonplace among followers of Christ. But just because the Mighty One can supernaturally provide food doesn't mean we are released from doing our part in food preparation. If you expect the Holy Spirit to supernaturally multiply your food every time you sit down at the dinner table or aim to feed the hungry, you and your guests may be in for some unplanned and unwelcomed hunger strikes.

Sustainable Living

The culture from which the Bible was written was predominately agrarian. Cultivating the soil, producing crops, and raising livestock was a way of life for most people and to some degree still is for much of the world. Mankind has worked the ground for millenniums, as our ancestors were farmers and ranchers who knew how to live off the land. Even Adam, the first man, was a gardener and zoologist by trade. Unfortunately, many of the skills of our fathers have been lost and forgotten in our generation.

We have become a society dependent on grocery stores and fast-food restaurants to nourish our bodies. Much of our diet comes from multiple and sometimes questionable sources. Buying prepackaged and processed food at the supermarket is a product of modern society. Most families in your community would be left vulnerable if supply lines were interrupted or if famine were to sweep the shelves of local markets. As we approach the end-times, perhaps it is time to re-teach ourselves some lost skills.

My wife and I have a small urban garden in our backyard, emphasis on small. It does not yield enough to replace our produce, provide an income or feed the homeless, but it does supplement our diets with organic fruits and vegetables in addition to providing hands-on lessons for our children. Though small, the revelation and fruit it has brought to our family has been huge, but our long-term goal is sustainability.

There's something grounding about working the same material that we were created from. As I till the very soil that produces my sustenance, I have observed both seedtime and harvest and been drawn into God's presence more than once. For some reason, I am able to hear the whispers of Heaven a bit more clearly in the garden. This makes sense considering the significance of biblical gardens like Eden, Gethsemane, and the Promised Land. I have found that the more in touch I am with the land, the more in touch I am with God's appointed times and seasons as well.

Since agriculture is the subject of many of Jesus' parables and is at the heart of much of the Bible's background, the more we understand the principles of the seed the more we can understand Scripture in context. Not only is farming and gardening a practical way to prep for the future and save at the grocery store, but it also is a spiritual act that bears unique fruit. It would benefit every serious student of God's Word to have a basic working knowledge of planting, cultivating, harvesting, weeding, sowing, and reaping. For this reason, there is value in brushing up on your gardening skills and finding your inner green thumb.

Debt

Carrying debt is a way of life for a lot people and is how most businesses operate these days. Being in debt, however, is not without its challenges, risks and drawbacks. Proverbs says, "The borrower is servant to the lender" (Prov. 22:7b), and "Do not agree to guarantee another person's debt or put up security for someone else" (Prov. 22:26 NLT). Solomon, who was one of the Bible's wisest and richest men, characterizes debt as a form of slavery and advises against putting up security for another.

Habakkuk weighs in on the subject as well, cautioning against loading up on creditors and using leverage to produce an income. He writes, "'Woe to him who increases what is not his—how long? And to him who loads himself with many pledges'? Will not your creditors rise up suddenly? Will they not awaken who oppress you? And you will become their booty" (Hab. 2:6b-7). In other words, borrowing money to make money can backfire.

Late-night infomercials preach that you should never risk your own money with investments. Instead, they advise risking the bank's money or taking a second loan on your house. This is problematic for believers because, when unable to repay, this practice has the potential to violate the law of love and discredit our witness. We are essentially gambling with another man's garment.

> *"If your neighbor is poor and gives you his cloak as security for a loan, do not keep the cloak overnight. Return the cloak to its owner by sunset so he can stay warm through the night and bless you, and the LORD your God will count you as righteous"* (Deuteronomy 24:12-13 NLT).

Taking risks with someone else's property is unwise and unloving. Any loss we experience becomes another's loss, especially when we don't have the means to repay what we promised we would. We should return out of love what has been loaned to us in faith. In this passage found in Deuteronomy, we are even called to prematurely return the collateral of what we are owed out of kindness to our debtor. Caring for someone else's property or money when it's in our possession, even if it belongs to the bank, is our spiritual obligation.

The Torah called for the cancelation of all debt in Israel every seven years. Additionally, each man's possession was returned to him in the Year of Jubilee. Notice it was not loan approval that was the cause for rejoicing but loan repayment. Life and joy and freedom are found in debt cancelation and living debt-free, not the other way around.

Financial debt is a major contributor to fear, so hear the word of the Lord. It is a G.O.O.D. word: Get Out Of Debt. Do everything in your power to get out of debt. You are not called to be a borrower but a lender to the nations, for "the LORD your God will bless you just as He promised you; you shall lend to many nations, but you shall not borrow…" (Deut. 15:6). If what we possess is not really ours, how will we lend to the nations with compassion?

This will likely require a lifestyle change. It will mean buying more things with cash than with credit. It will mean being comfortable living on less. It may take some adjustment, but it will be life-giving and advantageous for you in the long run.

Historically, those who have learned to live modestly fair much better in times of crisis than those who have been pampered. Folks of the working class are often more resilient than the privileged, simply because they have no sense of entitlement. Despair does not defeat the commoner as easily as it does the advantaged. Because they are not used to being spoon fed and know how to exercise restraint, their will remains unbroken and unfazed when they have to tighten the belt.

THE BULLET POINT

There are many ways to dodge a bullet, one of which is prophetic preparation. Though not our only recourse, preparing for what lies ahead is one way to respond in faith to God's Word. It also ensures that we position ourselves to be rescuers instead of those in need of being recued.

Psalm 91 implies that preparing for the inevitable and believing for the impossible are not incompatible. It readies us for the worst but leaves us expecting for the best. What it doesn't do is encourage apathy. Poor planning and shortsightedness are not honorable attributes, so don't let the times in which we live paralyze you into inactivity.

When gathering manna, "…he who gathered much had nothing left over, and he who gathered little had no lack" (Exod. 16:18). For Israel, those who prepared much were not over-prepared, and those who prepared little were not under-prepared. Regarding preparation, let's be gracious with one another. Those inclined to gather much should not look down on those who gather little and trust in God's supernatural provision for their lack. Those inclined to gather little should not ridicule those who by faith prepare by gathering much. Be convinced in your own mind and honor one another's faith. My philosophy is to do what you can do and leave the rest up to God. If we do our part, we can expect no less from Him.

Above all, refuse to be reduced to a survivalist mentality. The goal of life is not to outlive our neighbor or to preserve our own existence. Rather, the goal of life is to preserve the lives of others by laying down our lives for the gospel. Exchange a survivalist mentality for a revivalist mentality, and don't settle for being merely a survivor. Become an instrument of revival.

ENDNOTES

1. Several members of our fellowship were given specific directives about preparation. One intercessor was instructed to prepare physically and spiritually and to not stop until further notice. Another in our community dreamt of three fierce dark tornadoes coming to the land and was told to prepare for eight people. In her dream, she ran to her house for cover and found children taking refuge there. After boarding up the windows and instructing the children to sing praises to the Lord, the storm passed and all were safe. Meljoné had a series of gripping dreams. In one she was taken to a well-to-do neighborhood in a large urban city that was experiencing the aftermath of a devastating disaster. Many were displaced from their homes and took to the streets. As some families were feasting in their living rooms, others roamed the neighborhood scouring for food and shelter. Dreams can be highly symbolic and subjective, and dream language can be tricky to interpret. I have learned to hold dreams lightly unless given specific instructions from the Lord. I cannot say with certainty whether the visions of our community foresee future events, but we did feel they came in answer to our prayers. It was as if the Holy Spirit

was instructing us to listen up and place a marker on some of the prophecies that we had been exposed to.

2. D. Thomas Lancaster, *The Holy Epistle to the Galatians* (Marshfield, MO: First Fruits of Zion, 2011), 47-48.

3. See Matthew 24:6-8.

4. Ralph Waldo Emerson, accessed October 10, 2012, http://www.1-love-quotes.com/quote 48679.

5. Matthew Stein, *When Technology Fails* (White River Junction, VT: Chelsea Green Publishing, 2000), 1.

6. Mel Tari, *Like a Mighty Wind* (Green Forest, AR: New Leaf Press, 1971), 47-49.

CHAPTER 10

HIS ANGELS

*"For He will give **His angels** charge over you, to keep you in all your ways. In their hands they shall bear you up, lest you dash your foot against a stone"* (Psalm 91:11-12).

NOT COUNTING my wife, I have never knowingly seen an angel, but I once had a conversation with one on the telephone. It happened in 2003 during the first year of our marriage.

I was preaching at a youth event in Southern California, and it was the third night of the conference. The meeting went late, and I didn't return to my hotel until after midnight. I promised Meljoné that I would check in before I went to bed, so I called her on her cell phone. The phone rang several times, and about the time the voicemail usually picks up a voice answered. It was not my wife. It was a man.

He sounded about Meljoné's age at the time, maybe twenty-three or twenty-four years old, and he spoke to me in a Chinese-sounding, Asian dialect. Puzzled, I questioned, "Hello? Who is this?" He answered me, but I couldn't understand him. "Can I speak to my wife?" I said. By the way he responded to my questions it seemed he could comprehend what I was saying, but I hadn't a clue what he was saying. I continued, "Is Meljoné there? What's going on?"

What was even odder was that I could hear what sounded like serene instrumental music playing in the background and a woman reciting poetry. Her voice sounded similar in age to the man who answered the phone, and her poetry had the flavor of passages from the book of Song of Solomon. She was reciting one stanza in English and another in that same Asian-sounding language. As surreal as it was, her voice made me feel somewhat warm and comforted.

Needless to say, I was perplexed and a bit concerned. "What happened to my wife?" I thought. "Where could she be? She wouldn't attend a party this late without telling me, would she?"

The conversation continued for another thirty seconds with the same results, so assuming I had dialed the wrong number I hung up the phone. I decided to try our home line, and after a couple of rings Meljoné picked up.

"Hello," she answered in a groggy voice.

"Hi, baby. Did I wake you?"

"It's okay," she said. "How was the meeting?"

"Oh, it was awesome. Um, did you lose your cell phone?" I asked.

"No, it's in the living room. I think someone just tried to call me. I heard it ringing."

"It was me," I said and proceeded to tell her what happened. We thought perhaps I had dialed the wrong number but quickly realized I couldn't have since I used the speed-dial function on my phone. Besides, she heard her phone ring in the living room. "Oh, right," we agreed.

We were both a little baffled, but it was late. We brushed it off, figuring my call must have bounced off the wrong cell tower and gotten transferred to some mountain region of Tibet or to a nice Asian couple living in our apartment complex.

The next morning, however, the mystery thickened. Meljoné went into the living room and checked her phone. Someone had left a message on her phone and that someone was me! On it she heard me saying, "Hello? Who is this? Can I speak to my wife? Is Meljoné there? What's going on?" The recorded message lasted about a minute. She didn't hear the man speaking in Chinese or the woman reciting poetry, just my voice on the message.

This put a wrench in our theory. The call couldn't have gotten redirected to another number because my conversation left a message for her on her voicemail. This also ruled out that I may have dialed the wrong number or had been talking to someone else. It was clear that someone had answered Meljoné's phone that night and talked to me, and somehow only my voice was recorded on the voicemail.

I am convinced there were angels in our living room that night, and for some reason they answered my wife's phone. More evidence to this fact is that before I left for the trip I prayed over our apartment, stationing angels to guard over Meljoné while I was away. Additionally, Meljoné was spending time in prayer that night in the living room and felt that she was entertaining angels. The only logical solution is that my call interrupted an angelic party happening in our apartment that night while Meljoné slept. I only wish I had the sense to stay on the line a little longer, asking some specific questions. Maybe I could have gotten some clear direction for my life!

That being said, I learned a few things from that experience. One, angels are for real and apparently answer cell phones. Even when we are unaware of their activity or don't understand their speech, God still uses them to speak to us and protect us. Two, perhaps the angels sounded about Meljoné's age because they were her personal angels. Maybe they have been with her since birth. Three, my Filipino wife has at least two Asian angels who recite poetry!

MORE ARE WITH US

Scripture is filled with angelic accounts of deliverance. Lot was escorted out of Sodom by an angel. Peter was sprung from prison by an angel, while Daniel was protected by an angel when he was thrown into the lion's den. An angel assured Paul of his safety from an ensuing shipwreck, and it was an angel that warned Joseph in a dream to flee with Mary and young Jesus. In fact, an angel appears to Joseph in a dream several times in the first two chapters of Matthew.

The question we must ask is not, "Do angels really exist?" or "Do they protect us from danger?" Scripture clearly answers yes to both. The question we should pose is, "Will I trust that God will send His angels when I need them?"

In Second Kings 6, Elisha and his servant are surrounded by Syrian raiders carrying orders to assassinate the notorious prophet. Scripture records that Elisha comforts his friend, saying, "Don't be afraid. Those who are with us are more than those who are with them." After Elisha prayed, the servant's eyes were opened to the spiritual realm, where he saw the hills full of chariots of fire. The story recounts that a whole army of warring angels blinded the eyes of the marauders and rescued Elisha and his servant.

In Psalm 91, God promises to give us the ministry of angels that will both guard and guide us. If we could only just catch a glimpse of the unseen world, like Elisha's servant, we may see a host of Heaven surrounding us, declaring that "those who are with us are more than those who are with them" (2 Kings 6:16). What a confidence booster to know that no matter what gun barrel we are staring down, we're packing angels.

ANGELS ON THE MOUNTAIN

I belong to an accountability group that involves five good friends from my college days. Even though two live on the east coast and three of us are on the west coast, Scott, Erik, Derek, Les, and I have continued to stay in close contact with each other.

We have decades of history together. Over the years we've traveled overseas together, been in each other's weddings, and watched our children grow up.

We've gone on mission trips, attended conferences, read books, taken prayer retreats, and worshipped together. We continually seek to challenge each other in the Word, in habits, in purity, in relationships, in marriage, and in fatherhood. These lifelong buddies have been such a great source of joy and encouragement to me.

A couple years ago all five of us met up for a weekend of camping just outside Yosemite National Park. Two in our group had just turned forty, and they had a desire to "do something big" for their fortieth. Climbing Half Dome seemed big enough, so we all decided to conquer the sixteen-mile trek together.

As a boy, I hiked Half Dome with my father and my older brother, but I had forgotten how challenging of a climb it is. It is an all-day event, as it takes the average person eleven to twelve hours round-trip from the valley floor. The trail to Half Dome is as grueling as it is gratifying. Several miles of steep switchbacks and countless granite-blasted steps reward you with stunning views of magnificent waterfalls and beautiful high-country canyons.

Once you conquer a demanding quarter mile section called the Shoulder—this after nearly eight miles of treacherous hiking—you reach the base of the dome. The hardest challenge of the hike now confronts you, as you are greeted by sheer cables running straight up the smooth side of the rock. The challenge is less physical as it is mental. The cables can be quite intimidating when your feet are sore and your body is taxed. Some only make it this far, as your mind screams at you, "You're not going up that, are you? This is far enough, buster."

On the morning of the hike everything went smoothly enough. After setting up camp the night before, we woke up before dawn, drove to the trailhead, started out early, kept a good pace, summited the top before noon, and took some great pictures. But as can happen at elevations around 9,000 feet, the weather took a sudden turn for the worse.

Just after noon the wind picked up and thick clouds moved in, bringing dramatic temperature changes. We had just started our descent down the cables when a light sprinkle turned into a hailstorm. Visibility dropped considerably due to sticking fog and lightning became a legitimate concern.

Hiking Half Dome can be challenging enough in sunny weather, but in slippery, wet weather it can be extremely dangerous, especially when there are a lot of climbers on the mountain. This happened to be one of the first weekends of summer, so the trail was terribly busy and congested. Hundreds of climbers were still on the mountain as the wet granite started to feel more like a giant ice cube.

It is recommended that you wear gloves when navigating the hand cables, but of course that was the one item I forgot to pack. About halfway down the cables on the descent I almost lost my grip when one of the poles designed to anchor the cable to the mountain dislodged from its drilled hole above me. Now only attached by an eyelet, the heavy steel pole slid down the cable and crushed my hand against the pole below it. It took a nice chunk of skin out of my hand and index finger, but no way was I letting go of that cable.

As the hail began to fall, traffic on the cable portion slowed considerably. What normally is a fifteen- to twenty-minute pass through this section took well over two hours for some. Hikers clung white-knuckled to the cables, slowing up the entire line. Parents with small children were moving at a snail's pace. Some hikers were shouting obscenities to get others below them to keep moving, while others risked going outside the cables to get down the slope faster.

Erik, Les, and I had reached the bottom of the cable portion safely, but Scott and Derek had not yet descended. Unbeknownst to us, Scott and Derek were stuck on the cables in the wet and frigid conditions. Derek was feeling unusually weak and dazed on the way down, which we later discovered was altitude sickness. Keeping his balance was a challenge. Huddled under a tree to find shelter from the hail, we were a bit concerned since it had been more than two hours since we had last seen them.

As they were descending, Scott was helping Derek navigate the cables, but the long line of hikers was slowed by a terrified young woman wearing shorts and flip-flops. She had been abandoned by her boyfriend, and on several occasions had almost slipped and fell. Scott took the time to encourage her and assist her to the bottom of the cables, while at the same time managing to coach Derek to safety.

Miraculously, all three reached the bottom of the cables safely, but it was only a short while later that conditions grew even worse. The hikers stuck on the cables were growing weary, and the place where the post had come out of its mooring and smashed my hand was making it difficult for people to maneuver past. In their panic, some were being a little careless. And then it happened.

One man was negotiating around that section where my hand was injured when he slipped and lost his grip. Many heard him yell and watched in horror as he tragically slid hundreds of feet down the granite face to his death.

The mountain suddenly came to a standstill. Nobody moved. People began calling 911 from their cell phones. Emergency crews came by helicopter, and rangers had to escort the remaining hikers off the cables and down the mountain. It was well past midnight before the last hiker reached the valley floor.

That night we were exhausted and sobered. When we reached the trailhead, we each phoned our wives, as news of a forty-year-old man falling to his death climbing Half Dome was reported. Needless to say, our wives were relieved. As we all sat around a table in Curry Village eating pizza, our conversation was reflective. What if Scott had not been there to help Derek? How close was that girl to falling off the cables? What if we had been right next to the man when he slipped off? What if that steel pole had caused me to lose my grip?

But Derek reminded us about how we had spent a considerable amount of time in prayer that morning in the car on our drive into the park. We prayed for each other, for our families, and for angelic protection during our hike. As we looked back on that day, we thanked God for His protection and wondered how many angels had accompanied us on the mountain. I guess angels walk the trails of Half Dome, too.

ON ASSIGNMENT

Testimonies like these are not uncommon. We probably all have stories of when we should have fallen off that precipice or of missing a near accident, but what about the times we were unaware of Heaven's intervention? Hebrews says,

"Do not forget to entertain strangers, for by so doing some have unwittingly entertained angels" (Heb. 13:2). Since angels can seemingly appear as ordinary people, perhaps we've gone about our day oblivious to the activity of angels around us more than once.

This happened to me recently. I was walking into a restaurant with my wife to meet some friends for lunch when I was approached by a man for a handout. He took me by surprise because he was right at the entrance, dressed in fine clothing and didn't have the appearance of a typical street person. Although I had some cash in my wallet, I brushed him off and said, "Nah, man."

After returning home from lunch the man's face came to my mind in prayer. I felt convicted for lying and for not helping him. I had money, but I didn't have compassion. My policy is usually to buy a needy person a meal instead of straight up giving him money, but in this case I did neither. Would it have been an imposition to invite him to enjoy lunch with our pastor friends? Perhaps the Lord would have used us to minister to this gentleman, or maybe he would have ministered to us!

The Holy Spirit spoke to me in a still, small voice and said, "That man was an angel sent to test you." Gulp. I guess I failed that test. I had violated Luke 6:30, when Jesus says to, "Give to everyone who asks of you." After owning up to my actions, I vowed to be ready for the next test.

That day I learned a valuable lesson and also gained insight into the assignment of angels. Not only are they sent to protect us, they also minister to us in various ways. They can take on a human appearance and even wear nice clothing, and who knows? Maybe even sit down for lunch with us.

The best angel stories are reserved for Heaven. There, we'll get to see the story behind the story. No matter whether we are conscious of impending danger or not, perhaps we have been entertaining angels more than we realize, and maybe they have been interacting with us without our knowledge.

INTERVENTION

The truth is everyone needs angelic intervention from time to time, even the Son of God. After the devil tempted Jesus in the desert, Matthew records that "angels came and ministered to Him." (Matt. 4:11) On another occasion, Jesus was praying in the

> Perhaps we have been entertaining angels more than we realize.

garden of Gethsemane prior to His arrest, when "an angel appeared to Him from heaven, strengthening Him" (Luke 22:43).

If Jesus needed angelic strength for His life and ministry, how much more do we? Apparently, my wife needed the ministry of angels and so did our Half Dome hiking adventure. Here is our confidence: When we make the Lord our dwelling place, He promises to strategically place angels around us for our good in time of need.

> *"For He shall give His angels charge over you, to keep you in all your ways. In their hands they shall bear you up, lest you dash your foot against a stone"* (Psalm 91:11-12).

You may remember this was the same passage that Satan quoted when he prodded Jesus to throw Himself from the pinnacle of the temple.1 Not surprisingly, the devil misquotes it and misapplies it, leaving out "to keep you in all your ways." This phrase must be very important if Satan purposely omits it, and here is the truth he wants us to disregard: If we keep ourselves in all of God's ways, God will keep us in all of ours.

Abba once spoke to me, saying, *If you will take care of My business, I will take care of yours.* Applying this to this discussion, when we find ourselves in trouble and out of God's protection, it might be good to ask ourselves if we are keeping to the ways of God. Perhaps this is what the enemy wants us to forget.

On that day when the devil tempted the Lord, Jesus wisely didn't fall into his trap. Instead of deploying legions of angels, He made perhaps the most profound declaration about His identity, saying, "It is written again, 'You shall not tempt the LORD your God'" (Matt. 4:7).

Something similar happened with Jesus and Peter in the garden of Gethsemane. When Peter drew his scabbard and cut off the right ear of Malchus, Jesus rebuked him, saying, "Do you think that I cannot now pray to My Father, and He will provide Me with more than twelve legions of angels?" (Matt. 26:53). Even though He had thousands of angels at His disposal, Jesus refrained from marshalling them. He had unshakable trust in His Father's will because He lived in the secret place.

THE BULLET POINT

Angels are most often referred to in Scripture as *holy* angels, *the* angels or *an* angel. Once, Jesus even cautioned His disciples not to despise children, saying that *"their* angels always see the face of My Father who is in heaven" (Matt. 18:10b).

But here in Psalm 91 God promises to give *His* angels charge over us, as if these are a special class of angels that are *His* angels. Certainly all angels are His, but to those who stay close to Him He will see to it that His personal angels are dispatched on their behalf. It's always good to have angels watching over you, especially when they are *His*.

ENDNOTE

1. See Luke 4:10-11; Matthew 4:6.

CHAPTER 11

WILD BEASTS

*"You shall **tread upon the lion and the cobra**, the young lion and the serpent you shall trample underfoot"* (Psalm 91:13).

BLOOD, FROGS, lice, flies, pestilence, boils, hail, locusts, darkness, and death. Of the ten plagues of Egypt, nine directly affected or involved animals. The bloodied waters of the Nile destroyed the fish population. Frogs jumped out of the river and invaded the land. Dust became lice (or gnats). Swarms of flies covered the ground and air. Disease wiped out Egyptian livestock. Boils broke out on man and beast. Hail decimated the trees, vegetation, and wildlife. Armies of locusts turned the land dark, and even the farm animals suffered a death of their firstborn. We sometimes forget that just as people experience God's judgment, so do animals.

The fourth plague translated as swarms of flies is a product of modern scholarship, but many traditional interpreters understood it to be a plague of wild animals. Swarms of flies may indeed be the correct rendering, but it's also possible that the plague was of vicious and dangerous animals suddenly and without warning attacking the Egyptian people.

Judgment by way of animals is not without scriptural precedent. Ezekiel prophesied that Yehovah would send "four severe judgments on Jerusalem—the sword and famine and wild beasts and pestilence—to cut off man and beast from it" (Ezek. 14:21b). At the opening of the fourth seal, John writes, "I looked, and behold, a pale horse. And the name of him who sat on it was Death, and Hades followed with him. And power was given to them over a fourth of the earth, to kill with sword, with hunger, with death, and by the beasts of the earth" (Rev. 6:8).

Death at the paws of a predator is not the most honorable way to die. Poisonous snakes attacked the Israelites when they spoke against God and Moses. A lion killed the man of God who disobeyed the word of the Lord. Forty-two teenagers mocked Elisha and were promptly mauled by two mama bears. Jezebel's flesh was eaten by dogs after being thrown out the window in Jezreel. Daniel's accusers were cast into a den of lions, breaking all of their bones before they even reached the floor.

> Both animals and humans will be held accountable for the shedding of innocent blood.

What a contrast when we study the lives of the anointed. Samson defeated and tore apart a threatening lion with his bare hands. David not only killed a lion but also a bear to protect his sheep. Daniel survived a whole family of hungry lions, while Benaiah killed a lion in a pit on a snowy day. Paul was delivered out of the mouth of the lion and suffered no harm when he shook off a poisonous viper that had fastened onto his hand while building a fire on the island of Malta. Even Jonah was hurled out of the belly of a fish before being fully digested.

I don't know about you, but I don't plan on experiencing death-by-ferocious-animal. Being stung, eaten alive, or killed by a deadly cobra, scorpion, polar bear, piranha, crocodile, great white shark, box jellyfish, or brown recluse spider is not the way I intend to go out. I prefer to die in peace, and becoming lunch for some predator is not my definition of dying peacefully and painlessly.

THE ANIMAL KINGDOM

After the flood the relationship between man and animal changed. As God added meat to our diets, the fear of man fell on every beast, bird, and ocean animal. Upon exiting the ark, the Lord instructed Noah and his sons,

> *"For your lifeblood I will surely demand an accounting. I will demand an accounting from every animal. And from each man, too, I will demand an accounting for the life of his fellow man"* (Genesis 9:5 NIV).

The Great Judge will hold all of His creation accountable, both animals and humans, for the shedding of innocent blood. This means that murderers will not fare well on this planet. It also means that wild beasts will not attack a person without a cause, and if they do their Creator will require a reckoning for their actions.

As Kingdom custodians, we understand that the Kingdom of Heaven dominates all earthly kingdoms, including the animal kingdom. We have been given authority over the beasts of the field, the beasts of the air, and the creatures of the sea and have no cause to fear that which we are anointed to rule.[1] Jesus said that His followers would "take up serpents" and not be harmed (Mark 16:18). He also gave them "authority to trample on serpents and scorpions, and over all the power of the enemy, and nothing shall by any means hurt you" (Luke 10:19). He demonstrated this when He was with the wild animals in the wilderness and was protected by angels.[2]

This authority came in handy for me once on a ministry trip to Thailand. A team of college students and I were staying at a missionary's house in Chiang Kham when I decided to go for a run through the village. The neighborhood where the house was located was in a small community on the edge of town. It was nighttime, and I thought a run under the stars would be a nice way to get some much-needed exercise.

Jen, one our team members, joined me and after returning from the outskirts of town, the local dogs noticed us as we jogged back into the village. One barking dog joined another, and soon a pack of spirited dogs were chasing us down the main dirt strip. I was more than a little concerned that we would not make it back to the house, but then I remembered the words of the Master, "Nothing shall by any means hurt you." I promptly turned around, pointed at the dogs and commanded them to back off and shut up. To our amazement that's exactly what they did. "Wow, this authority stuff works," I told Jen.

Dutch Sheets tells the story of a minister who had made it his habit to begin each day with an hour of prayer. One morning he felt urged to pray longer so he prayed for another hour. After two hours he still felt the need to continue, so he prayed yet another hour, interceding for others and asking for protection and blessing over his day. After three hours of prayer, he went on about his day.

That evening as he was mowing the lawn, he felt something repeatedly brush up against his leg. When he looked down he saw an agitated rattlesnake coiled up and ready to strike. It lunged to strike him but missed his leg and merely brushed up against it. For some reason the rattler was disoriented and unable to strike his target. Although snakes do have poor eyesight, this was unusual. Those three hours of prayer must have activated the shield of God's presence and placed an invisible but tangible force field around him.[3]

STEALTH MODE

"A thousand may fall at your side, and ten thousand at your right hand; but it shall not come near you" (Psalm 91:7).

Antoine Augustin Calmet, a French monk, translates this verse, "A thousand enemies may fall upon thee on one side, and ten thousand may fall upon thee upon thy right hand, but they shall not come near thee to take away thy life."[4] Perhaps one the reasons calamity misses us is because that which seeks to strike us may not have the ability to see us. God chose to blind the eyes of the Syrian army when they were sent to assassinate Elisha and his servant. He may well do this for us. Whether debilitating the senses of a coiled rattlesnake or making us invisible to a night-stalking predator, it is His presence that keeps us hidden in stealth.

Stealth technology was first designed and developed in the U.S. by engineers at Lockheed Aircraft Corporation. The F117 Nighthawk with its sleek design and radar-absorbent coating paved the way for armed forces to effectively mask military aircraft.

What makes stealth aircraft so effective is that it is equipped with faceted surface designs and a unique composite coating that can absorb and deflect radar signals. In addition, specialized electronics can be installed that enable the airplane to confuse enemy monitoring systems. Stealth aircraft not only have the technology to elude detection from tracking systems but also have the ability to cloak themselves from guided missiles.[5]

Living under the shadow of the Almighty is much like stealth technology. God's presence serves as a cloaking device that shields us from the fiery missiles of the enemy, deflecting and confusing their strike. The Almighty clothes us with a holy and divine camouflage, painting us with the blood of Christ and absorbing the blows for us on the cross. It's as if we become indestructible and invisible to certain attacks that others fall prey to.

WILDLIFE REFUGE

Our authority over animals does not give us license to misuse or abuse them. Quite the opposite, actually. With any authority comes the responsibility to rightly exercise that authority. When God gave Adam dominion over every living thing, it came with a responsibility to care for what he had been entrusted with. "A righteous man regards the life of his animal" (Prov. 12:10a). Cruelty to pets or maiming, torturing, and killing animals for sport is contrary to Kingdom values and is an abuse of our God-given authority.

The Sovereign God chose man to steward His creation for a reason. Of all His created beings, only we have been given the necessary ingenuity, intellect, organizational skills, and communication capabilities to care for the earth.

Humans are like no other species. Our speech communication is vastly different and superior to anything observed in animals, making us alone the proper creature fit to look after nature. Whether we accept it or not, we cannot deny that the well-being of the planet rests in our hands. Being created superior to plants and animals should not give us cause for condescendence but rather a sense of conscientiousness.

One time I was cleaning out the garage when a hummingbird flew inside and got trapped in the garage with me. It kept flying to the top of the ceiling, looking for an exit, but was unable to fly under the door to find its escape. I wanted to help the bird without hurting it, so I prayed, *Father, help me to help it.* I thought to grab a broomstick and extend it toward the frantic bird. Surprisingly, it landed on the end of the stick almost immediately and clung to it. I slowly inched the broomstick toward me and gently clutched the bird. I was expecting it to squirm and peck at my hand as I held it, but it remained completely still. I carried it out of the garage and released it, and we both went merrily about our day.

Protection from dangerous animals goes with the territory of Psalm 91, but our citizenship in the Kingdom also gives us the anointing to protect animals from any dangers they may face. Just as God is our refuge, so we can be a refuge for wounded or disadvantaged animals.

There is coming a day when our relationship with the animal kingdom will be restored to what it once was. Isaiah prophesies that one day "the wolf also shall dwell with the lamb, the leopard shall lie down with the young goat, the calf and the young lion and the fatling together; and a little child shall lead them" (Is. 11:6). In addition to His bride, even the behavior of wild animals will come under the rest and reign of Christ in the Millennium.

LIONS, SNAKES & DRAGONS

"You shall tread upon the lion and the cobra, the young lion and the serpent you shall trample underfoot" (Psalm 91:13).

In ancient times, when an enemy was defeated the victor placed his foot on the neck of the prostrated foe. "Treading underfoot" became a metaphor for dominion and victory. As stated, Psalm 91 affirms that we have gained victory over dangerous beasts and have dominion over venomous animals.

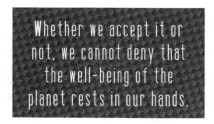

It is no mistake, however, that Psalm 91 mentions the lion and the cobra by name. They are two of the most feared animals known to man, but it's what they personify that should interest us. The serpent and the lion are descriptive depictions of the devil.

Satan came as a serpent to deceive Eve. John identifies the serpent as the one "who deceives the whole world" (Rev. 12:9), and he describes seeing an angel who "laid hold of the dragon, that serpent of old, who is the Devil and Satan, and bound him for a thousand years" (Rev. 20:2).

The devil is also likened to a lion. Peter exhorts, "Be sober, be vigilant; because your adversary the devil walks about like a roaring lion, seeking whom he may devour" (1 Pet. 5:8). John writes, "Now the beast which I saw was like a leopard, his feet were like the feet of a bear, and his mouth like the mouth of a lion. The dragon gave him his power, his throne, and great authority" (Rev. 13:2).

A third depiction of the devil found in these verses is—the dragon!

The history of dragons is an ominous study. Found in almost every culture are myths and legends of dragons, with dragons often holding major spiritual significance in religions around the world. Some dragons are depicted as symbols of destruction and evil; others as keepers of the universe. Some are winged, fire-breathing reptiles that dwell in lairs and guard hidden treasure; others are sea creatures possessing wisdom and capable of human speech.

The Slavic dragon is a three-headed serpent that spits fire. The Chinese dragon possesses magical powers and is revered as the highest ranking animal in the animal hierarchy. In Japanese and Korean cultures, dragons are depicted as water serpents that rule over wells, rivers, and rainfall. The Indians, Persians, Celtics, and Vietnamese all have their own tales of dragons, and the Greeks and Romans used them as military emblems on their shields.[6]

In a collection of third-century anecdotal folklore written by Claudius Aelianus, a species of dragons once inhabited Ethiopia and had a lifespan that rivaled most animals. It hunted elephants and could grow to a length of 180 feet.[7] Likewise, in the old English poem, Beowulf, the hero and mighty warrior Beowulf defeats the cave-dwelling, fire-breathing dragon while suffering a mortal wound in the process.

Where do dragons come from and who inspired these tales? Are dragons spiritual entities, mythical monsters, or simply descriptions of prehistoric animals such as dinosaurs?

The identification of Satan as a dragon is uncovered in the book of Revelation. "War broke out in heaven: Michael and his angels fought with the dragon; and the dragon and his angels fought, but they did not prevail..." (Rev. 12:7-8). "The dragon was enraged with the woman, and he went to make war with the rest of her offspring, who keep the commandments of God and have the testimony of Jesus Christ" (Rev. 12:17). "Then I saw another beast coming up out of the earth, and he had two horns like a lamb and spoke like a dragon" (Rev. 13:11).

The popularity and glorification of dragons in our culture is disturbing to me. We have dragon books, dragon art, dragon fish, dragon fruit, dragon festivals, and dragon tattoos. For kids there are dragon toys, games, helmets, cartoons, costumes, balloons, stuffed animals, and action figures. Marketers put dragons on our drinks and dragons on our clothes. They introduce dragons as magical creatures to our preschoolers and depict dragons as heroes in our movies. My hatred for dragons grows daily. In fact, I think I'm even starting to develop some hard feelings toward Puff.

John calls Satan a "dragon, that serpent of old." You wonder what the serpent looked like before it was given its dust-eating curse in the garden. We know it was wiser than any other animal and evidently could talk. It must have been taller and had legs as well. Add wings and fire to its breath and you get all the depictions of a dragon. Perhaps the serpent of Eden was less snake in form and more dragon in appearance.

It's not surprising that some scholars prefer to translate the word "serpent" as *dragon* in Psalm 91:13. From this we can extract a demonic reference to the verse, conveying that we have supernatural dominion over the devil in addition to natural wildlife. When Paul wrote that he "fought wild beasts in Ephesus" (1 Cor. 15:32 NIV), it's not likely he was wrestling alligators or referencing the gladiator games. He was referring to his struggle against vicious men and quite possibly demonic principalities.

DEMONIZED AND DRUNK

I have had my fair share of demonic confrontations over the years. One happened in the summer of 1997 when I was on a prayer mission in North Africa with some colleagues. While sitting in an outdoor café drinking mint tea and sharing the gospel with a young man named Hassan, two severely deranged men kept walking by our table. Both had that crazed look in their eye and seemed to stare me down with each pass. One would spy on us from a couple tables away and mumble something under his breath.

After making several passes, he finally stopped, put his face in mine and spoke some angry words to me in Arabic. Katie, a friend and team member who was with me, immediately grabbed my knee from across the table and started praying in the spirit.

It was obvious this man was demonized. One look into his eyes would convince anyone of that fact. Unfortunately, he was also drunk, as I could smell alcohol on his breath. In that moment, I thought, "What have we gotten ourselves into this time? As if being demonized isn't enough? This lunatic is demon-possessed and drunk!"

I did something similar to what I did with those dogs in Thailand. (Okay, so I have one go-to move.) I stood up, pointed to the man and shouted, "Do you want to be free?" I figured the man probably wouldn't understand my words in English, but I knew those demons would. When I said it, the man's face lit up as if he saw the most terrifying ghost. He flung his body backwards, knocked over a table, scattered some chairs, and ran off frantically down the street. I was tempted to blow the end of my finger and return it to its holster like it was some western shootout at the town's saloon. The incident would have been comical if the spiritual atmosphere wasn't so intense.

When I sat back down my heart was racing like a sprinter on caffeine. Katie's wide eyes stared back at me from across the table. The waiter came by and nonchalantly picked up the table and chairs. As for our new friend Hassan, he didn't skip a beat. Uninterrupted, he waxed long about his life for another hour as if nothing out of the ordinary had happened. By the grace of God, we shared the full gospel with Hassan and left him with one of the twelve Arabic Bibles we had smuggled in to the country. We soon would discover that these kinds of crazy run-ins with demons were the norm for that entire two-week expedition.

THE BULLET POINT

Some of the world's most dangerous animals are also some of the smallest. In fact, most of the dangers you and I face, whether demonic or not, are largely unseen—carbon monoxide, secondhand smoke, radon exposure, electromagnetic radiation, E. coli, malaria, polio, and smallpox. An invisible enemy is usually the most lethal.

The end-times will be marked by an increase in demonic activity and animals acting strangely. Don't be surprised if you see wildlife displaying aggressive behavior as the Day approaches. As you rest in the secret place of the Most High, rest assured that the Father of Creation will protect you from any and all demonized beasts. Psalm 91 gives us the confidence that no matter what kind of predator we may face, human or non-human, there is a presence with us more powerful than the one that comes to assault us.

So, the next time you find yourself surrounded by a pack of ravenous dogs, confronted by a coiled rattlesnake, or swimming in shark-infested waters, be at ease. You are not leaving this world having been mauled by a tiger or digested in the belly of a bear. Speak to the animal and exercise your authority over the situation. Come out of your prayer closet clothed in the confidence of His protection and knowing the authority you have in His name.

ENDNOTES

1. See Genesis 1:26-30.

2. See Mark 1:13.

3. Dutch Sheet, *Intercessory Prayer* (Ventura, CA: Regal Books, 1996), 80-81.

4. Adam Clarke, *Clarke's Commentary* (Electronic Database, Biblesoft, 1996).

5. Encarta Encyclopedia 2000, Microsoft Corporation, 1993–1999.

6. Ibid; "The History of Dragons," accessed August 8, 2012, http://www.draconika.com/history.php; "Dragon History – Ancient Accounts,", accessed August 8, 2012, www.allaboutcreation.org/history-of-dragons-faq.htm; Wikipedia contributors, "Dragon," Wikipedia, The Free Encyclopedia, August 7, 2012, http://en.wikipedia.org/w/index.php?title=Dragon&oldid=506178587.

7. "Drakon Aithiopikos," accessed August 8, 2012, http://www.theoi.com/Thaumasios/DrakonesAithiopikoi.html; "Aelian," accessed August 8, 2012, http://www.britannica.com/EBchecked/topic/7081/Aelian.

CHAPTER 12

BULLETPROOFING YOUR WORLD

"No evil shall befall you, nor shall any plague come near your dwelling" (Psalm 91:10).

THIS CHAPTER is a collection of prayers and prophetic acts that can be used to declare God's favor and protection over your home, marriage, children, travel, health, business, ministry, and finances.

BULLETPROOFING YOUR HOME

In Chapter One I recount the story of the prophetic act Meljoné and I performed when we purchased our first house. I highly recommend doing something similar where you live. Pounding stakes into your yard and pouring oil on the ground, however, is not the only way to bulletproof your dwelling place.

Anointing Walls

We anoint the walls of our home often. Depending on how much traffic and guests we receive, sometimes we need to pray through our house a couple times a week. If you notice increased warfare in your home, you may want to sweep it clean spiritually. We've also found it beneficial to pray through the house after a troubling or demonic dream. Be sure to uproot any deposit made and close every portal opened by the dream or demonic attack.

Instructions: Grab some anointing oil (olive oil will work, too) and touch each inside wall of your house. I pray something along these lines:

> *"Lord of Heaven and Earth, I submit this home and the household that it represents to You and to Your Kingdom. I declare that You are Lord and King of this home, and we come under Your authority and protection. I take up the authority I possess as father and husband of this family, and I now bless what You've entrusted to me.*

> *"Let this oil represent Your Word, Your Spirit, and Your blood. Refresh, revive, revitalize, reenergize, refuel, reload, and refill us. Cover us, Father. Protect us and hide us under the Shadow of the Almighty.*

> *"I declare that this house will stand and be unharmed in the midst of any and all natural or supernatural disasters, including floods, fires, earthquakes, volcanoes, hurricanes, tornadoes, and mudslides. I cancel all evil plots and assignments against us and declare that this house will not be the victim of robberies, thefts, home invasions or break-ins. Thwart the plans of the enemy and make us invisible to every threat.*

> *"I take authority over every spirit that contends with the Kingdom of Heaven in this house, including but not limited to fear; doubt; unbelief; anxiety; worry; stress; anger; frustration; infirmity; religion; rebellion; rejection; Jezebel; manipulation; control;*

witchcraft; generational, familiar and familial spirits; division; contention; miscommunication; and [add your own]. I bind these, in the name of Yeshua of Nazareth. I bind your hands, feet, eyes, ears, and mouth. You are gagged and straightjacketed. You can't move, operate, traffic, look, listen, speak, or in any way function in this place. I cast you out of here and away from here. You will not affect anybody who lives or visits this home, and you will go to where Jesus Christ sends you and no where else. I loose the fruit of the Spirit, the love of God, the Kingdom of God, the glory of God, the favor of God, and the presence of God in this place."

Communion

Serving communion in your home is a powerful prophetic act. We take it together as a family weekly during our Sabbath meal or when we need an extra push in the Spirit. There have been seasons where I've incorporated communion into my morning prayer time. Communion is also beneficial when a special breakthrough is needed, like when warring against cancer or witchcraft.

Doorpost Declarations

Scripture instructs us to write God's laws "on the doorposts of your house and on your gates" (Deut. 6:9). The word for doorpost here is *mezuzah*. To fulfill this command, many Jews and believers today hang a decorative box known as a mezuzah on their door frames. Rolled up inside this protective case is a piece of parchment inscribed with the Shemah or other Scripture verses. This box also provides a visual and spiritual reminder that "as for me and my house, we will serve the LORD" (Josh. 24:15).

Of course there are other ways to fulfill this ordinance. Affixing a mezuzah is just one way. Some have found great benefit in hanging framed Scripture passages in their entryway and above their doors. Others write Scripture passages on the floors and walls of their home during construction or before/after a fresh coat of paint.

Threshold Prayer

This prayer is a legal document and can be used to create a spiritual boundary at the threshold of your home, especially if your house is used for ministry or as a house-church. This is designed to be printed out, rolled up like a scroll, and attached above the front door or entrance of your home.

> *"I declare that this property, established by legal boundaries, and all that is under or within the spiritual and/or legal stewardship and authority of this house, are set apart unto Christ, His will and His Kingdom rule and dominion. As measured according to His will, these boundaries are established: As it is in Heaven, His Will, His Presence and His throne, including its foundation of righteousness and justice.*
>
> *"All who cross this threshold enter into the above mentioned Embassy of the Kingdom of God, and by so doing come into implied and willing submission to the Sovereign Will and government of God.*
>
> *"Therefore there will be:*
>
> - *No sin*
>
> - *No sickness or disease*
>
> - *No death*
>
> - *No demonic influence, oppression, interference, or assault*
>
> - *No curse*
>
> - *No false gods, false idolatry, or rebellion to the will of God within these Kingdom Embassy boundaries that will remain.*
>
> *"All demons are subject to Christ who has been given all authority in heaven and earth and under the earth. Upon crossing this threshold, all spirits are subject to every command given to them by those who come under the covering of this household. There will be*

no backlash, retaliation, or transferring of spirits to the building or any of the members of this family, extended family, or their possessions. I decree that as a Kingdom Embassy no information will leave this building or flow out through any person that will be used to empower the enemies of God and His Kingdom. There will be no access in or out by watching spirits or any other spirit or human assignment set against the work of the Kingdom of God or the testimony of Yeshua Messiah. All who come in defiance of the Kingdom of God or in defiance of this decree over the threshold come as thieves and robbers and yield to the judgment of God for that defiance.

"Those who willingly cross this threshold will come under the anointing of the Holy Spirit that brings conviction of sin leading to repentance and will hear and receive the good tidings of salvation, deliverance, healing, restoration, liberty, and comfort. They will receive 'beauty for ashes, the oil of joy for mourning and garments of praise for the spirit of heaviness that they may be called trees of righteousness, the planting of the Lord that He may be glorified.'

"'And they shall rebuild the old ruins, they shall raise up the former desolations, and they shall repair the ruined cities, the desolations of many generations' (Is. 61:3-4)."

(See Isaiah 61:1-4; Ezekiel 40–48; Matthew 8:14-17; 10:7-8; 28:19; Luke 10:8-9, 17-20; 11:2-4; Philippians 2:5-11; Colossians 1:9-23; 2:9-15; Revelation 1:7-18; 22:6-21.)

Strategic Land Prayer

This is a prayer of repentance and a declaration of liberty for you, your family and the land you inhabit.[1]

"Father God, I come to You, the Creator of heaven and earth, the Holy One who revealed Yourself to Israel as YHWH (Yehovah), the eternal I AM—the covenant-keeping God. I acknowledge that You are the only true God, the Supreme God of Gods, and King of Kings. I believe that You have revealed Yourself through Jesus Christ who came in the flesh, died on the cross, rose from the dead and ascended to heaven to sit at Your right hand on the throne. I enter now into Your Presence through the way Jesus Christ opened by the sacrifice of Himself on the cross and come before You in His Name. I confess that all are saved by faith through the work of Jesus Christ on the cross and not by works, and that my salvation was a gift from You. I submit myself under Your authority as the Judge who has the power to forgive sin and bring healing.

"I come before You today in confession and repentance on behalf of myself, my ancestors, and this land to ask You to break the power of sin in my life and the lives of my people (tribe/clan/ethnicity). I honor my earthly father and mother, all ancestors of my flesh and blood and those who have inhabited this land before me, but I reject their sin and turn my back on it. I forgive them for the effect of their sins on my descendants and on me. I confess and reject all my own sins and ask You to allow the Holy Spirit to apply the power of the blood of Jesus Christ shed on the cross in my life and to release the victory of the cross over sin and bondages in my life as well as those of my descendants. I also ask You to allow the Holy Spirit to apply the power of the blood of Jesus Christ over Satan and all his hosts of darkness. I believe through faith that the victory is available right now. You, King of Heaven, are the same yesterday, today and forever. You are the Alpha and the Omega. You are the beginning and the end; who was and is and is to come.

"I now utterly renounce anything of the past as having any right of entrance or influence upon my future or upon this property. I

declare in the spiritual realm and upon the earthly realm that my inheritance, my descendants, my children, my marriage, my office, and all that I identify with as steward of what God has entrusted to me is turned completely and unreservedly to the Lord and to His destiny and future. I release it to Him for all He chooses to do with it."

Idolatry

"I confess that my ancestors and I and those who have inhabited this land before me were involved in the sin of idolatry. I now reject and renounce all forms of idolatry.

"I reject and renounce the worship of images made of wood, stone, gold, bronze, or any other material.

"I reject and renounce the worship of sacred pillars, poles, obelisks, statues, or any other forms of ba'al worship as well as the worship of standing stones, trees, or any other similar objects.

"I reject any sense of self-idolatry and supremacy over other people that my family may have expressed as part of their inheritance or right.

"I reject and renounce all myths, legends, and stories about gods and spirits and also all incantations that are used by any nature worship and the worship of creation in the sun, moon, stars, planets, or the earth itself.

"I reject and renounce any gods and spirits worshipped in my culture that I do not know, and I list those names I do know and renounce them by name (allow the Holy Spirit to speak to you here). I now turn my back on those gods and in the Name of the Lord Jesus Christ ask that they be made the footstool of the Lamb of God.

"I reject and renounce all forms of animal worship or totems. I sever all soul ties with the animal kingdom and every animal worshipped in my culture—including all forms of superstition involving animals.

"I reject and renounce all worship and charming of snakes, serpents, dragons, or any other water spirit or spirit of fire.

"I reject and renounce all worship of plants in my culture, including the witchcraft use of plants as medicines. I cut myself and my family loose from all magic powers, secret formulas, medicines, false healing, and healing powers introduced from the East that is empowered by the physic realm and brings no glory to Jesus Christ. In the Name of Jesus Christ, I cut myself, my ancestors' and descendants' names free from any person, gods, or evil forces, that would use our names to bring us under their power and authority.

"I reject and renounce any allegiance I, my family, or those who have lived on this land—past or present—have ever made with any ancient spirit finding its origin in either the spirit of paganism or the spirit of humanism as found in Genesis 3 and 11. I therefore reject and renounce all forms of ancestral worship, including ceremonies and rituals at ancestral tombs and graves—even when fashioned in the form of a monument honoring my ancestors. I state that there will be no more idol worship in my family lineage.

"I reject and renounce all forms of worship of my nationality or national emblems of my country. I reject and renounce any self-centeredness, self-exaltation, self-seeking of pride in human accomplishments. I also reject any form of rebellion against God's authority that has taken place at any time by any member of my ancestral lineage—past or present.

"I reject and renounce all forms of exclusiveness, including those of any secret society or organization that excludes membership of certain people and would suggest that they have the hidden truth not revealed to infidels.

"I reject and renounce all forms of ideologies and arguments in my culture that have exalted themselves against the knowledge of God.

"I ask forgiveness for every ungodly sprinkling and incense burning in temples of idols and reject and renounce those as practices of Satan and idol worship. I reject and renounce any altars to idols whether it is images, ideas, or ideologies. In so doing I cut off soul ties—and those of my family—with any priests, priestesses, temples, or places of worship as well as all worship rituals and ceremonies with idols. I totally renounce and cut myself free—and my family—from all superstition and any and all observances and remembrances of special days, seasons, and ceremonies performed for idols in my culture.

"I reject and renounce any belief in incantations and formulas, as well as rituals and prayers during burials that are not centered upon Jesus Christ, who is the Way, the Truth, and the Life.

"In the name of Jesus Christ, I cancel all curses, charms, incantations, magic, and witchcraft done against us in the name of any spiritual force. I take us out from under the mastery of Satan, the cosmic universe or any document, and I place us under the Lordship of the One True God.

"I petition for protection for myself, my descendants, and my family against any spiritual force still worshipped by my family, people of my culture, or people of this land through ceremonies, rituals, or observances."

Bloodguilt

"I confess that my ancestors and I and those who have inhabited this land before me have been involved in the sin of bloodshed. I accept the guilt of this sin on behalf of myself, my family, and the people of this land.

"I confess, reject, and renounce all shedding of blood at illegal altars to idols or spiritual forces, whether the blood of animals or humans.

"I confess the sin of bloodshed in abortion and acknowledge that it is murder and the shedding of innocent blood, and I reject this practice.

"I confess, reject, and renounce any bloodshed through murder or killings done in time of war that I or my ancestors were involved in, whether through defense or attack.

"I confess the sin of committing land clearances and the removal of innocent people from their own land. This is nothing less than the shedding of innocent blood and the breaking of covenants. Much of this involved immorality and rape of the land and its people. The theft of property, dignity, and freedom of people took place. I acknowledge on behalf of myself and my family that this involved the sin of usury, exploitation, control, manipulation, and intimidation. I confess, reject, and renounce this sin committed before God and His people over every generation in my family lineage originating from Adam and Eve to the present—so that I, my family, and our descendants will never again be held responsible. May the violation that has affected both the spiritual realm as well as the physical realm be removed under the blood of Christ.

"I confess, reject, and repent of any bloodshed through manipulation, tattoo, scarification on my body, or any body piercing done in opposition to the guidelines of Scripture.

"I confess, reject, and repent of any drinking or eating of blood done in my culture on my part or that of my ancestors—whether wittingly or unwittingly; whether as part of a covenant ritual or a fraternity rite—even if it included the incorrect use of the Sacrament of Holy Communion. I confess, reject, and repent of any rituals involving blood, any documentation signed in blood, or any ceremonies where my ancestors or I used blood. I confess, reject, and repent of any blood covenants made with spiritual forces, people, or animals.

"I forgive anyone who has committed bloodshed against me, my family, or my people. In the Name of Jesus, I ask that the blood of Jesus silence the voices of blood crying out against my family and me. I ask that the cycle of violence and bloodshed stop and that no more revenge will be required. I ask that the mourning of the land caused through untimely bloodshed on the past of my family lineage will end now and the healing of land under the influence of my ancestral line will take place."

Immorality

"I confess that my family and I and those who have inhabited this land before me have been involved in the sin of immorality. I confess, reject, and renounce any form of perversion in the lives of my ancestors or myself—the sin of incest in the family, intercourse outside of marriage, adultery, homosexuality, bestiality, masturbation, fornication, premarital sex; prostitution, pornography, sexual abuse of any form, rape, the uncovering of my own or anybody else's nakedness in perversity, and any other form of uncleanness in my thoughts through watching x-rated movies or movies with explicit sex scenes or through reading books. I ask forgiveness for any illegitimate births that have taken place within my family lineage. I break the curse of illegitimacy over my descendants and myself until the tenth generation.

"I recognize that my involvement in sexual sin has contributed to a spirit of violence in the land and confess and repent of this activity. I forgive anyone who was involved in violating my body, thoughts, or emotions through sexual assault. I ask now that the blood of Jesus Christ cleanse my body and soul from any memories, thoughts, wounds, or emotions."

Broken Covenants

"I confess the sin of broken treaties in the lives of my ancestors and myself and those who have inhabited this land before me. I confess, reject, and renounce the practice of divorce. I now ask for forgiveness for the involvement in the breaking of marriage vows, and I forgive all marriage partners in my ancestral lineage for breaking covenant within their marriage partners in any place and at any time. I forgive them for the effect this has had upon my life as well as the lives of my descendants.

"I now choose to cut my descendants and myself free from the curse of broken covenants. I confess, reject, and renounce any broken covenants or treaties my country, my clan, or my people were involved in whether with God or with another culture or people.

"I confess, reject, and renounce any broken covenants my family or I committed in business and in every way that this has affected the national and international arena. I ask for restitution to take place as under the timing and direction of God whenever and wherever necessary. I confess, reject, and renounce any contribution I had to the breaking up of my family at any time in the past or present, and forgive anyone else who was involved in such a way."

Proclamation

*"In the Name of Jesus Christ of Nazareth and with the authority
that I have as a believer in Him, I now declare that I and this
property have been redeemed out of the hand of Satan and all
idolatry; I am cleansed of this sin and through His blood I am
forgiven, sanctified, cleansed, and justified. I now turn my back
on all forms of idolatry, take my territory back from Satan, and
tear up any contracts made with him.*

*"I cut my descendants and I free from all oaths, blood bonds, and
soul times with every person who was involved in any of the above.
I ask for a total removal of all guilt and shame on my descendants
and me for whatever sin we have been involved in. I now strip
ancestral gatekeepers of their authority in my lineage and in
my spheres of authority, and ask You, Lord Jesus, to destroy
all ungodly keys. May all papers of commission be torn up and
these to be totally decommissioned. In the Name of Jesus Christ,
I ask that You will now please close all evil doors and seal them
permanently with Your blood. I declare that according to Isaiah
22:22 that whatever doors You close will never be opened, and
whatever doors You open will never be closed.*

*"I declare over my ancestral lineage—past, present or the future—
that the psychic door in our bloodline be permanently closed under
Jesus Christ who holds the key to life and death and resurrection.*

*"I ask forgiveness for myself and the involvement of my ancestors
with all the above-mentioned and confess that it is an abomination
in Your sight. I thank You, Father, that You will never remember
these sins and that You will remove them as far as the east is from
the west. In the Name of Jesus Christ, I now command every evil
spirit to leave me immediately and all idols to come under God's
judgment. I pray that all curses on the land that exist due to my
sin and the sin of my ancestors be broken and nullified in the*

Name of Jesus Christ and that the land be set free from my sin, the sin of my forefathers, and the sin of their parents.

"I declare the release of Your blessing upon the land—ecologically and economically and in every level of security; from personal to national to international; and for the release of innovation and creativity upon the land—in keeping with Leviticus 25:23-24. May the full redemption of the land be brought forth in a manner that reflects Your glory and honor. May it release destiny into our lives and the land You have entrusted to us.

"Lord Jesus Christ, I ask You to send the reviving power of Your Spirit in to our families, our churches, our communities, our cities, our counties, our territories, and our nations. Nothing is impossible for You, and by faith we release the power of Your reviving power in the areas of ecology, economy, banking, commerce, industry, politics, ethics, morality, health, education, as well as the rekindling of Your bride as the prophetic mouthpiece of God in society today, speaking no longer with unrighteousness and compromise, but instead with authority and righteousness."

BULLETPROOFING YOUR MARRIAGE

Husband

"Great and Glorious Father, I commit to You my wife and the covenant we have made together. May our union be rooted and grounded in Your love and be the foundation that makes this family strong. Your Son said in Matthew 19:6, "What God has joined together, let not man separate." I ask You to guard our commitment, our intimacy, our eyes, and our trust. Keep our passion for each other alive and thriving. Protect us from divisive words, divisive behavior, divisive attitudes, factions,

wedges, and those who seek to separate us. Uproot, reveal, and heal all anger, bitterness, resentment, frustration, walls of separation, and emotional pain that may exist, whether known or unknown, within this marriage. May we truly be one in the spirit and one flesh. Keep us unified in the bond of peace and help our communication grow deeper, kinder, and more pleasing in Your sight. Carve out for us special times of laughter, joy, and memories that solidify and intertwine our lives, hearts, and families with each other. Give us vision for our marriage and an identity beyond child rearing.

"Abba Father, thrill my wife with Your love and passion for her. May she be ever captivated by Your ways of kindness. Keep her close to Your heart, Your voice, and Your conviction. Wash her, cleanse her, and refresh her in the water of Your Word. May she be full of wisdom, insight, discernment, knowledge, understanding, and revelation in the ways of truth. I declare that she is a Proverbs 31 woman full of the power and fruit of the Spirit. She will not be a controlling woman like Jezebel but will submit, honor, respect, and love those whom You have placed as an authority over her life. I declare that she is more than a conqueror, a woman of strength who will not bow to manipulation, temptation, control, or gossip. Protect her from all tricks, traps, schemes, and tactics of the enemy, including but not limited to—depression, loneliness, insecurity, vanity, bitterness, disease, and [add your own]. Give her eyes for her husband and protect her from all who seek to use or abuse her. Woo her into the secret place through Your love, and may she find her identity and rest in You. Let my leadership encourage her to spread her wings and shine forth her beauty to the world around her.

"As her husband, I spread the corner of my garment over her as my wife and cover her spiritually, physically, emotionally, mentally, and financially. Teach me how to love her as Christ

loves the church and to care for her as I would care for my own body. Help me to lead by example and exemplify what it means to be a man of God. May I find joy in pleasing her, listening to her, loving her unselfishly, humbling myself, preferring her needs above mine, honoring our marriage vows, accepting her family as my own, and fulfilling her destiny in Christ. Give me eyes for her and her alone. Keep her as the delight of my eyes, and may I always appreciate her beauty, her opinion, and her perspective. Put a muzzle over my mouth when I am angry and want to speak words that damage her, and guard me from embarrassing her or exposing her faults in public. Thank You for bringing this woman of God into my life and for calling me to serve her with my life. She is Your daughter, and may I never take her or our marriage for granted."

Wife

"Great and Glorious Father, I commit to You my husband and the covenant we have made together. May our union be rooted and grounded in Your love and be the foundation that makes this family strong. Your Son said in Matthew 19:6, "What God has joined together, let not man separate." I ask You to guard our commitment, our intimacy, our eyes, and our trust. Keep our passion for each other alive and thriving. Protect us from divisive words, divisive behavior, divisive attitudes, factions, wedges, and those who seek to separate us. Uproot, reveal, and heal separation, all anger, bitterness, resentment, frustration, walls of separation and emotional pain that may exist, whether known or unknown, in this marriage. May we truly be one in the spirit and one flesh. Keep us unified in the bond of peace, and let our communication grow deeper, kinder, and more pleasing in Your sight. Carve out for us special times of laughter, joy, and memories that solidify and intertwine our lives, hearts, and families with each other.

Give us vision for our marriage and an identity beyond child rearing.

"*Abba Father, thrill my husband with Your love and passion for him. May he be ever convinced of Your faithfulness. Keep him close to Your heart, Your voice, and Your conviction. May Your Word dictate his thoughts and actions, as he is a light to those around him. Fill him abundantly with wisdom, insight, discernment, knowledge, understanding, and revelation in the ways of truth. I declare that he is a man of humility, courage, loyalty, integrity, and full of the power and fruit of the Spirit. He will not be controlling or domineering but will lead by example and servanthood. I declare that he is more than a conqueror, a hard worker who provides for his family, and spends time with us. Protect him from all tricks, traps, scheme,s and tactics of the enemy, including but not limited to—pride, depression, loneliness, insecurity, lust, pornography, anger, disease, and [add your own]. Give him eyes for his wife. May he run from temptation as Joseph did with Potiphar's wife and be invisible to the plans of seductive women. May he be so fulfilled in You that no other pleasure or beauty can lure him away from it.*

"*As his wife, I willingly choose to honor, respect, and love him as my husband and spiritual covering. Teach me how to submit to his leadership and be a helper to him. Teach me to trust his leadership, allow him to lead, and to be an example to him of what it means to be a woman of God. May I find joy in pleasing him, listening to him, loving him unselfishly, humbling myself, preferring his needs above mine, honoring our marriage vows, accepting his family as my own, and fulfilling his destiny in Christ. Give me eyes for him and him alone. Keep him as the delight of my eyes, and may I always appreciate his strength, his advice, and his perspective. Put a muzzle over my mouth when I am angry and want to speak words that damage our relationship, and guard me from disrespecting him in public. Thank You for bringing this man of God into my life and for calling me to serve him with my life. He is Your son, and may I never take him or our marriage for granted."*

BULLETPROOFING YOUR CHILDREN

I like to pray this over my children each night before they go to bed. Time may not permit you to pray the full prayer, but at a minimum I recommend declaring the "Prayer of Blessing" every night.

Prayer of Blessing

"[Yehovah] bless you and keep you and make His face to shine upon you and be gracious unto you. The Lord lift up His countenance upon you and give you peace. I bless your body, soul, and spirit. May He make you like Ephraim and Manasseh." (See Numbers 6:22-27; Genesis 48:20.)

Prayer of Protection

"I ask You, Father, to hide them in the shelter of the Most High. May they find refuge under the shadow of Your wings. Keep them invisible to the plans of the enemy.

"Place Your hand of protection over them from evil and those who would mean to harm them. Foil the plans of the enemy. I ask You to protect their innocence and purity."

Prayer of Health

"I declare no sickness, disease, bug, cold, flu, infection, infirmity, virus, or illness will come upon them in any way, shape, or form.

I ask You to keep them far from H1N1, whooping cough, fever, allergies, germs, and harmful bacteria. I declare that they will not have sore throats, runny noses, headaches, ear infections, coughs, stomachaches, nausea, broken bones, or broken teeth. I break off all generational disease and patterns of sickness, including cancer, heart disease, high blood pressure, diabetes, and [add your own] in the name of Yeshua of Nazareth.

"Heavenly Father, I ask You to keep their immune systems strong. May their calcium and iron levels be perfect. May their teeth come in straight, strong, and painlessly, and I declare that they will not have cavities or require braces."

Prayer for Spiritual Vitality

"I break all generational, familial, and familiar spirits over them, including but not limited to fear, doubt, unbelief, anxiety, worry, stress, anger, frustration, infirmity, religion, rebellion, rejection, Jezebel, manipulation, control, witchcraft, and [add your own].

"I ask that they would walk in love, joy, peace, patience, kindness, goodness, gentleness, faithfulness, self-control, integrity, and humility. May they be hungry and passionate for the things of God and for His Word. Give them wisdom, insight, discernment, knowledge, understanding, and revelation.

"May they be full of courage, strength, boldness, and faith, yet humble, obedient, and submissive to authority and to their parents. May they grow up with a love for the Lord, His Word, truth, and others. May they find hatred for all that is sinful, perverse, unclean, and demonic.

"Father, I ask You to visit them in the night season with dreams, visions, angelic visitations, and heavenly encounters. Reveal to

them at a young age who You are and who You have called them to be. May they come to know You and be filled with the Holy Spirit at a young age."

Prayer for Parents

"Grant us, as parents, the wisdom to rear and disciple these children in the things of God. Show us what You have called them to be and help us to shape them into Your will for their lives. May their destiny in Christ be fulfilled. We release them to You, for they belong to You. Thank You for entrusting us with these precious gifts."

BULLETPROOFING YOUR TRAVEL

Auto

"Heavenly Father, I ask that You give us safety on the roads. May there be no accidents, injuries, car problems, engine failures, running out of gas, or flat tires. I ask You to protect us from swerving cars, impaired vehicles, or animals that may run out onto the highway. I now station angels to travel with us, to go before and behind us, above and below us, to the right and left of us, protecting us. Keep me sober and alert as I drive, and grant me wisdom to make wise driving decisions as I seek to obey all traffic laws."

Air

"Heavenly Father, I declare that this airplane is not going down unexpectedly. I ask You to keep the pilots sober, alert, and wise during this flight. If there are any potential engine problems

*with this flight, may they be detected and fixed before we take off.
I ask You to foil and frustrate any plans of terrorism or ideas of
hijacking for this flight. I also declare that my luggage will be on
my flight and will not get lost, damaged, or stolen in transit."*

BULLETPROOFING YOUR HEALTH

*"Father in Heaven, I thank You that I am fearfully and
wonderfully made. All Your works are marvelous, including my
body, and I now present my body to You for healing. As I heed
Your voice and obey Your commands, I trust that You are Yehovah
Rapha, my Healer. No sickness can stand before You, for You are
the creator and healer of this body.*

*"According to Psalm 103:3, You forgive all my iniquities and heal
all my diseases. Let Your Word bring truth to my body and to this
affliction. The facts may show sickness, but the truth is that Christ
bore my grief and carried my sorrows and by His stripes I have
been made whole. Let the Sun of Righteousness arise over me with
healing in His wings. According to Philippians 2:10, every knee
must bow before the Lord Jesus Christ, including sickness and
disease. I speak to this body, take authority over it, and command
it to line up with the Living Word of God. I thank You that the
same spirit that raised Christ from the dead dwells in me and will
quicken my mortal body.*

*"I pray as Jesus taught us to pray. Let Your kingdom come and
Your will be done, on earth as it is in Heaven. Since sickness is not
a part of Heaven, I declare it has no place in my body or in the
Kingdom of Heaven. Disease and pain will not be my inheritance.
Plague and pestilence will not affect me or my household. I declare
no sickness, disease, bug, cold, flu, infection, infirmity, virus,
illness, or [add your own] will come upon me in any way, shape,*

or form. Where it has, it must leave. I ask You keep coughs, fevers, allergies, germs, and harmful bacteria far from me. I declare that I will not have sore throats, runny noses, headaches, ear infections, coughs, stomachaches, nausea, broken bones, broken teeth, or cavities. I break off of me all generational disease and patterns of sickness, including cancer, heart disease, high blood pressure, diabetes, allergies, and [add your own] in the name of Yeshua of Nazareth. Infirmity, affliction, disease, pain, and all manner of illness must leave me now.

"Heavenly Father, I ask You to keep my immune system strong and active. I command it to line up with the Word of God. It will fight off all disease and perform as it is designed to. Let Your truth permeate every cell of my body, from the top of my head to the soles of my feet. Father, cover me, protect me, and rescue me from every attack of the enemy. As in the days of Moses and Pharaoh, so shall it be with me. Plague, whether Heaven-sent or hell-vomited, will not come near my dwelling, for my dwelling is with the Lord.

"I rejoice at Your promise of divine health and ask You to keep me strong and disease-free all the days of my life. May Your abundant life guard my body, soul, and spirit until Your appearance."

(See Psalm 139:14; Exodus 15:26; Isaiah 53:4-5; Malachi 4:2; Romans 8:11; Matthew 6:10.)

BULLETPROOFING YOUR BUSINESS

"Heavenly Father, I commit this business and company into Your hands. I recognize that You are my employer and my provider, and I am utterly dependant upon You to give success to the work of my hands. Lead me, guide me, and direct my business decisions to most glorify You and serve those I do business with. As an owner, executive, manager and/or boss, help me, to disciple and

mentor unto Christ those who work over me, with me and under me. Grant me prophetic dreams and favor like Joseph, wisdom and understanding like Daniel, and prosperity like Abraham and Solomon. I ask for favor from Heaven that brings favor on earth. Anchor this company to be in the right place at the right time. Grant us contracts, visibility, interest, influence, and loyal customers whom we can be a blessing to. Open up new markets, ventures, and opportunities for us and give us creativity to fill a need in the market. Protect us from wrongful lawsuits, dishonest dealings, unwise decisions, and unscrupulous business practices. May our efforts yield a hundred-fold increase so this business can be a channel of blessing to many people and for generations to come.”

BULLETPROOFING YOUR MINISTRY

“Gracious Father, I declare my utter dependence upon You for this ministry. You have called me into ministry, and I trust that You will lead me and guide me according to Your will. Help me to never forget that my first ministry is always unto You. Like the five wise virgins, may my lamp always burn for You and for Your courts, and help me to seek You for those whom I am called to minister to.

“I admit my inabilities and recognize that without You I can do nothing. It is not by might or power or my experience or my prayers, but by Your Spirit. Unless You build this house, I labor in vain. I depreciate my flesh and appreciate the Spirit of God within me. May You increase as I decrease, and let there be less of me and more of You. As Your representative and ambassador, grant me brokenness, humility, faith, boldness, freedom, and joy. Call intercessors to pray for this ministry, and as we sow to Heaven let us reap on earth. Silence the mind-sets that oppose

Your truth, pull down the high and lofty pride that raises itself up against the knowledge of God, and plow through the tricks, traps, schemes and tactics of the enemy. I take authority over fear, doubt, unbelief, religion, pride, witchcraft, mockery, cynicism, accusation, distraction, confusion, Jezebel, Leviathan, and Babylon that would try to come against this ministry and our appointed times of ministry. I blind the spying third eye and close every sound or light portal it may have opened.

"Anoint me to preach and teach Your Word with boldness and humility. May I be ready in season and out of season. Strengthen me to patiently and graciously convince, rebuke, and exhort those with ears to hear. Toughen my skin and soften my heart as I endeavor to speak the truth in love. Like Samuel, may none of my words fall to the ground, and like Stephen may my opponents not be able to argue with the wisdom and Spirit by which I speak. Anoint my hands to serve, my eyes to see, my ears to hear, my feet to run, and my heart to give.

"Fill me with the Holy Spirit and fire. Ignite in me the fire of purity, passion, power, prayer, and praise. Mark me with Your presence and set me aside for Your glory. Send me out into Your harvest fields. Give me the anointing that breaks the yoke. Increase Your prophetic and evangelistic anointing on me, and activate the gifts of the spirit in me to supernaturally love others. Help me to hear Your voice and have Your heart. Lead me down Your paths of righteousness, and may I be sensitive to the moving of the Spirit. Show me the direction You are moving in that I may move with You. Open my eyes to see what You are blessing so I can bless it, and alert me to what the enemy is doing so I can oppose it. May I weep when You weep, laugh when You laugh, love what You love, and be grieved by what grieves Your heart. I declare that You have given this ministry the mind of Christ, and may You be seen and glorified through us.

"I ask for fruit, more fruit and much fruit. I thank You for the fruit You have given us, and may the fruit of this ministry be lasting and genuine. Open effectual doors for us and for the gospel. Provide the necessary finances to accomplish the vision and rebuke the devourer that seeks to dry up that provision. Grow us, teach us, mature us, and fashion us as a weapon in your hand. Send us Pauls to learn from, Timothys to mentor, and Barnabases to encourage and be encouraged by. Surround us with leaders filled with wisdom. Raise up an army through us who are full of faith, compassion, and perseverance and are anointed and appointed for this hour.

"I break off all backlash, retaliation and trailing spirits that would seek to attack my family. Protect them from all spiritual warfare. Cover them in Your blood and hide them under the shadow of Your wings."

BULLETPROOFING YOUR FINANCES

"Father, I come humbly before You, the Maker of Heaven and earth, the Creator all things seen and unseen, present and still yet to come. The earth is Yours, and all its fullness, the world and those who dwell in it. With You there is no lack, for every beast of the forest is Yours, and You own the cattle on a thousand hills.

"As I join my value system to Yours and place my resources in Your economy, I ask You to shower favor, blessings, and increase upon me so I have more than enough to co-labor with Heaven and see Christ receive His full reward. I ask You to bless the work of my hands, for it is Your plan to prosper and not harm me, to give me a hope and a future. My delight is in Your Word, so let whatever I do prosper and find success. I declare that You have ordained me to be the lender and not the borrower, the head and not the tail,

as I heed Your commandments. Since every good and perfect gift comes from above, I will continually thank You for every blessing that overflows in my life.

"You love a cheerful giver. Place it upon my heart to give freely and extravagantly from a cheerful heart to those You have placed along my path. As I do, I ask You to bless me in all my work and in everything I put my hands to. May it go well with me as I conduct my affairs with integrity and justice.

"I commit to bringing all my tithes and offerings into Your storehouse. May my gifts rise before You as a fragrant offering and be remembered before Your throne. Open the windows of Heaven and release abundant blessings as You promised You would. Throw open Your floodgates and pour out so much blessing that I will not have room enough for it. Your Word says that the faithful will abound with blessings, and the generous will prosper. Return to me a good measure, pressed down, shaken together, and running over into my lap. May I have such abundance that I can be generous on every occasion.

"Rebuke the devourer for my sake, O Lord, and surround me with Your favor as a shield. As I sow to Heaven may I reap to earth. Let my sowing lead to reaping and my weeping turn to joy. As I give generously, may I be given a generous portion in return. As I prove myself faithful with little, entrust me with as much as I can handle.

"Give us this day my daily bread. You are the one who gives bread to the eater and seed to the sower, and as I seek first Your Kingdom and righteousness, add unto to me all that I need. May You provide for the needs of my family and for those You have placed under my care. You will not allow the righteous to be forsaken or their children begging for bread. You are the one who supplies all my needs according to Your riches and glory in Christ Jesus.

"I trust, declare and believe You for:

- *Jobs and job offers*
- *Positions and promotions*
- *Provisions and resources*
- *Raises and bonuses*
- *Benefits, sales, and commissions*
- *Estates and inheritances*
- *Interests and income*
- *Rebates, refunds, and returns*
- *Checks in the mail*
- *Gifts and surprises*
- *Favorable settlements*
- *Finding money*
- *Debts paid off*
- *Expenses decreased and revenues increased*
- *Blessing and increase*
- *And storehouses unlocked.*

"Protect me from the sins of greed, avarice, and the love of money, which is the root of all kinds of evil. Grant me wisdom to steward and manage what You have entrusted to me, and help me to never make a decision based on finances alone. Free me from all poverty mind-sets, deficiency mentalities, and any spirit of lack that I may possess or that has been passed down to me through my ancestors. May I not be given too much to where I forget You, nor given too little to where I am desperate and dishonest.

"I declare that neither I nor my descendants will bow their knee to Mammon. Money will not control or manipulate us. Forgive me for allowing myself to go into financial debt. Free me from any and all servitude to my lenders as I seek to pay off this debt. Remove this mountain of debt that I am under, and may the only debt that remains outstanding is the debt of loving one another.

"You are the one who gives me the power to get wealth. Thank You, Father, for meeting all of my financial needs that I may have more than enough to give to the Kingdom of God and promote the gospel of Jesus Christ.

"Now to Him who is able to do immeasurably more than all we ask or imagine, according to His power that is at work within us, to Him be glory in the church and in Christ Jesus throughout all generations, forever and ever! Amen."

(See Psalm 24:1; 50:10; Jeremiah 29:11; Psalm 1:3; Deuteronomy 15:6; 28:12-13; James 1:17; 2 Corinthians 9:7; Malachi 3:10; Proverbs 28:20; 11:25; Luke 6:38; Malachi 3:11; Psalm 5:12; Matthew 25:21, 23; 6:11; Isaiah 55:10; 2 Corinthians 9:10; Matthew 6:33; Psalm 37:25; Philippians 4:19; 1 Timothy 6:10; Proverbs 30:7-9; Luke 16:13; Habakkuk 2:6-7; Proverbs 22:7; Romans 13:8; Deuteronomy 8:18; Ephesians 3:20-21.)

ENDNOTE

1. By Alistair Petrie, adapted and edited for this book.

ABOUT JEFF ROSTOCIL

JEFF was raised in a godly home in Northern California and is the youngest of four children. Before the age of three he was miraculously healed of three separate conditions and at the age of five met Christ while praying with his mother in the backseat of the family station wagon.

It wasn't until his college years that Jeff sensed God's call to full-time ministry. After graduating from San Jose State University with a business degree, he served for five and a half years at Butte College and Chico State University as a campus pastor. During that time he saw many devote their lives to Christ and be launched into ministry. He also was asked to preach and lead several evangelistic teams overseas to Thailand, Morocco, India, Europe, South America, China, Hong Kong, and most recently, Africa, Mexico, Argentina, and the Middle East.

Currently, Jeff travels as an evangelist speaking to adults and youth, both nationally and internationally. He is an excellent communicator with a genuine passion to know and share Christ. His messages are fresh and relevant, stirring God's people toward genuine revival, unity, and spiritual awakening.

Jeff founded SoleQuest International in 2002 and went on to earn a master's degree through Wagner Leadership Institute.

For booking, contact:

SoleQuest International
http://sqint.org
Office Phone: 925-963-4665

IN THE RIGHT HANDS, THIS BOOK WILL CHANGE LIVES!

Most of the people who need this message will not be looking for this book. To change their lives, you need to put a copy of this book in their hands.

> *But others (seeds) fell into good ground, and brought forth fruit, some a hundred-fold, some sixty-fold, some thirty-fold* (Matthew 13:8).

Our ministry is constantly seeking methods to find the good ground, the people who need this anointed message to change their lives. Will you help us reach these people?

> *Remember this—a farmer who plants only a few seeds will get a small crop. But the one who plants generously will get a generous crop* (2 Corinthians 9:6).

EXTEND THIS MINISTRY BY SOWING
3 BOOKS, 5 BOOKS, 10 BOOKS, OR MORE TODAY,
AND BECOME A LIFE CHANGER!

Thank you,

Don Nori Sr., Founder
Destiny Image
Since 1982

DESTINY IMAGE PUBLISHERS, INC.

"Promoting Inspired Lives."

VISIT OUR NEW SITE HOME AT
WWW.DESTINYIMAGE.COM

FREE SUBSCRIPTION TO DI NEWSLETTER

Receive free unpublished articles by top DI authors, exclusive
discounts, and free downloads from our best and newest books.
Visit www.destinyimage.com to subscribe.

Write to: Destiny Image
             P.O. Box 310
             Shippensburg, PA 17257-0310

Call: 1-800-722-6774

Email: orders@destinyimage.com

For a complete list of our titles or to place an order
online, visit www.destinyimage.com.

Made in the USA
Las Vegas, NV
28 June 2023

73995238R00108